the cooking lite feeling right cookbook

From the Home Economists of the Hunt-Wesson Kitchens

PUBLISHED BY POCKET BOOKS / FIRESIDE   NEW YORK

contents

Another *Original* publication of POCKET BOOKS/FIRESIDE

 POCKET BOOKS, a Simon & Schuster division of
GULF & WESTERN CORPORATION
1230 Avenue of the Americas, New York, N.Y. 10020

ISBN: 0-671-41778-9

First Pocket Books printing October, 1980

10 9 8 7 6 5 4 3 2 1

A
NORTON SIMON INC
COMPANY

SUNLITE® is a registered trademark of HUNT-WESSON FOODS, INC.,

POCKET and colophon are trademarks of Simon & Schuster.

Printed in the U.S.A.

introduction

Come, enjoy the "Lite" approach to feeling right with Sunlite!

Sunlite Oil has created a lot of excitement among consumers because it reflects today's desire for light eating and exercise. Exercising is fun, exciting and can be shared with friends and family. Eating wisely takes a bit of preplanning for meals, shopping and cooking, but the rewards of a feeling of well-being are worth it. Consumer enthusiasm was contagious, so our Home Economists blended the goodness of sunflower oil with our twenty years of experience to develop the recipes in this, our latest cookbook.

The "Cooking Lite—Feeling Right" cookbook is filled with over 150 quick and easy dishes and imaginative ways to please you, your family and your friends. The recipes included here were designed to fit today's life-style with its limitations of time, smaller households and appreciation of delicious, nutritious foods.

Our Sunlite recipes reflect a "lite" approach to cooking without giving up delicious eating. It simply suggests a more sensible way of preparing some of the foods you enjoy most—in a "Lite-er" way. We have taken some of your favorite old-time recipes, preserving the good flavor but updating them to meet the demands of today's contemporary family.

Whenever possible we avoided heavy creams, frostings, and large quantities of sugar or salt. We replaced solid fat and butter in recipes with Sunlite Oil, which contains no cholesterol, is low in saturated fat and is high in polyunsaturates. We steamed or sautéed your favorite vegetables to retain more of the vitamins and minerals, and included a wide array of fish and poultry recipes for healthier eating.

Lite cooking and physical activity go hand-in-hand. Walk to the train or bus, take the stairs rather than the elevator, bike out to the picnic grounds and join the kids in some of their outdoor activities; get a periodic physical checkup—eat light—get enough sleep—and watch your energy go up.

Use and enjoy our "Cooking Lite—Feeling Right" cookbook and walk, run, bike, skate or dance your way to a "feeling right" life!

DIRECTOR, CONSUMER SERVICES

appetizers and more

Tantalizing finger-foods for casual entertaining

won ton triangles *(illustrated opposite)*

Savory morsels to tempt your guests

450 g	1	(16-oz.) can bean sprouts, drained
240 g	1	(8½-oz.) can crushed pineapple, drained
110 g	1	(4-oz.) can water chestnuts, drained and diced
125 ml	½	cup chopped green onion
340 g	1	(12-oz.) pkg. won ton wrappers
		Sunlite Oil
		Oriental Dip (p. 37)
		Ketchup

In a bowl, combine bean sprouts, pineapple, water chestnuts and green onion; toss to mix. Place 1 rounded teaspoon of mixture in center of each won ton wrapper. Fold two opposite corners together forming a triangle. Moisten edges of skin to seal. Fill a heavy kettle or wok ⅓ full with Sunlite Oil. Heat to 350°F and maintain temperature with deep-fry thermometer. Fry a few filled triangles at a time, 1 to 1½ minutes until crisp and golden. Use Oriental Dip or ketchup as a dipping sauce. Makes 52 appetizers.

Note: Make ahead and freeze until ready to fry.

chimichangas

Serve with salsa, sour cream and guacamole

450 g	1	lb. pork shoulder, cubed
	1	onion, chopped
	1	clove garlic, minced
		Sunlite Oil
15 ml	1	Tablesp. chili powder
5 ml	1	teasp. seasoned salt
1 ml	¼	teasp. cumin
110 g	1	(4-oz.) can diced green chilies
60 ml	¼	cup water
	10	(9-inch) flour tortillas, warmed
375 ml	1½	cups shredded Monterey Jack cheese

In a large skillet, sauté pork, onion and garlic in 3 tablespoons Sunlite Oil over medium heat. Add chili powder, seasoned salt, cumin, green chilies and water; simmer, covered, 5 to 10 minutes. Place equal portions in center of each warm tortilla; top with cheese. Fold sides and ends of tortilla over to enclose filling. Secure with toothpick. Meanwhile, fill a Dutch oven or heavy kettle ⅓ full with Sunlite Oil. Heat to 350°F and maintain temperature with deep-fry thermometer. Fry chimichangas in hot oil 3 to 5 minutes until crisp and golden. Cut in half crosswise to make 20 appetizers.

tortilla chips

Irresistible treats

Sunlite Oil
1 doz. corn tortillas, cut in 1-inch triangles

Fill a large saucepan or electric skillet ⅓ full with Sunlite Oil. Heat to 350°F and maintain temperature with deep-fry thermometer. Fry a few tortilla pieces at a time until crisp and golden, about 3 minutes. Remove with slotted spoon; drain on paper towels. Store chips in plastic bag to retain crispness. Makes about 2 quarts.

Nachos: Spread tortilla chips in shallow baking pan. Sprinkle with 2 cups shredded Cheddar cheese. Broil for 3 minutes or until cheese melts. Makes 6 to 8 servings.

deviled eggs *(illustrated page 4)*

Great for picnics too

	8 hard cooked eggs
60 ml	¼ cup Sunlite Mayonnaise (p. 15)
15 ml	1 Tablesp. sweet pickle relish
5 ml	1 teasp. prepared mustard
1 ml	¼ teasp. seasoned salt
1 ml	¼ teasp. paprika
.5 ml	⅛ teasp. pepper

Cut eggs in *half* lengthwise. Remove *yolks;* combine in a small bowl with *remaining* ingredients. Mix until well blended and smooth. With a spoon or pastry tube, fill center of each egg white. Sprinkle lightly with additional paprika. Chill, covered. Makes 16 deviled eggs.

bettinas

Hot from the oven in a minute

375 ml	1½ cups <u>each</u>: shredded Monterey Jack cheese and Cheddar cheese
250 ml	1 cup Sunlite Mayonnaise (p. 15)
125 ml	½ cup sliced green onions
450 g	1 lb. loaf sliced cocktail rye bread

In a bowl, combine cheeses, mayonnaise and green onion; mix thoroughly. Spread on bread slices. Sprinkle with *additional* green onion slices, if desired. Arrange on cookie sheet. Broil 4 inches from heat 1 to 2 minutes, until cheese melts. Makes 40 to 45 Bettinas.

shrimp on the half shell

Elegant sit-down first course

125 ml	½	cup Sunlite Oil
60 ml	¼	cup fresh lemon juice
60 ml	¼	cup vinegar
10 ml	2	teasp. capers
8 ml	1½	teasp. seasoned salt
5 ml	1	teasp. dill weed
3 ml	½	teasp. dry mustard
3 ml	½	teasp. garlic powder
450 g	1	lb. shrimp, cooked, shelled and cleaned
	4	ripe avocados, halved and peeled
		Boston lettuce

In a bowl, combine first eight ingredients; mix well. Add shrimp; toss to mix. Marinate in refrigerator, covered, several hours. Stir once or twice. To serve, arrange avocado halves on bed of lettuce. Drizzle a little of the marinade over avocados. Top *each* with equal portions of shrimp and marinade mixture. Makes 8 servings.

cheese on a stick

Melt-in-your-mouth delicious

180 ml	¾	cup prepared biscuit mix
60 ml	¼	cup cornmeal
15 ml	1	Tablesp. sugar
	1	egg, beaten
125 ml	½	cup milk
450 g	1	lb. Cheddar cheese, cut in 1 × 2-inch pieces
		Sunlite Oil
	16	wooden or bamboo skewers

In a small bowl, combine biscuit mix, cornmeal, sugar, egg and milk; mix thoroughly. Allow batter to stand about 30 minutes. Fill deep-fry pan or Dutch oven ⅓ full with Sunlite Oil. Heat to 350°F and maintain temperature with deep-fry thermometer. Pierce cubes of cheese on ends of skewers. Dip in batter to coat cheese on all sides; fry in hot oil until golden brown. Drain on paper towels. Makes 16 appetizers.

Use the same batter for other on-a-stick appetizers: mushroom caps, pieces of frankfurter, zucchini slices, mozzarella cheese cubes, green pepper squares, etc.

mandarin "drummettes" *(illustrated page 4)*

Tasty conversation starter

	14	chicken wing "drummettes"
60 ml	¼	cup cornstarch
	1	egg, beaten
30 ml	2	Tablesp. milk
3 ml	½	teasp. seasoned salt
		Sunlite Oil

With a sharp knife, scrape and push meat to one end of the bone so it resembles a small drumstick. In a bowl, combine cornstarch, egg, milk and seasoned salt; mix until smooth. Set aside. Fill a heavy kettle or wok ⅓ full with Sunlite Oil. Heat to 350°F and maintain temperature with deep-fry thermometer. Dip "drummettes" in egg mixture. Add, a few at a time, to hot oil; fry about 5 minutes until golden brown. Serve with soy sauce or Oriental Dip (p. 37), if desired. Makes 14 appetizers.

Cut chicken wings at joints to make 3 pieces; Reserve tip and middle piece for stock.

With sharp knife push meat to one end of bone.

paper-wrapped chicken

Make ahead and freeze for parties

180 ml	¾	cup soy sauce
125 ml	½	cup honey
60 ml	¼	cup Sunlite Oil
60 ml	¼	cup white wine
3 ml	½	teasp. each: garlic powder, ginger and dry mustard
900 g	1½	to 2 lbs. boneless chicken breasts, cut into bite-size pieces
	25	(4-inch) squares of aluminum foil

In a bowl, combine all ingredients *except* foil; mix thoroughly. Marinate 1 hour. Place 2 to 3 pieces in center of each foil square; fold over to form triangle; double-fold edges to seal. Bake at 400°F 15 minutes. Makes 25 appetizers.

Note: Thread 5 or 6 chicken pieces on skewers; broil or grill 4 to 5 inches from source of heat 6 to 8 minutes. Turn and baste often with marinade. Makes 12 kabobs.

chilies con queso

Serve with bread cubes, chips or vegetables

250 ml	1	cup minced onion
30 ml	2	Tablesp. Sunlite Oil
25 ml	4 to 5	teasp. flour
375 ml	1½	cups milk
750 ml	3	cups shredded Cheddar cheese
250 ml	1	cup shredded Monterey Jack cheese
110 g	4	ozs. cream cheese, softened
110 g	1	(4-oz.) can diced green chilies
56 g	1	(2-oz.) jar pimiento, chopped

In a heavy saucepan, sauté onion in Sunlite Oil until tender. Stir in flour. Blend in 1½ cups milk; bring to boil. Cook, stirring until thick and smooth. Remove from heat. Add *half* <u>each</u>: Cheddar, Jack and cream cheeses. Cook and stir over low heat until cheeses melt. Repeat with *remaining* cheeses. Cook and stir until melted. Add green chilies and pimiento. To serve, keep warm on warming tray or in fondue pot. Makes 10 to 12 servings.

zucchini torte

A cheesy Italian delight

	1	small onion, chopped
	1	clove garlic, minced
30 ml	2	Tablesp. Sunlite Oil
125 ml	½	cup milk
	2	eggs, slightly beaten
125 ml	½	cup prepared biscuit mix
3 ml	½	teasp. Italian seasoning
3 ml	½	teasp. salt
.5 ml	⅛	teasp. <u>each</u>: pepper and paprika
	2	medium zucchini, quartered and thinly sliced
225 g	½	lb. Cheddar cheese, shredded
	1	Sunlite (9-inch) unbaked single crust (p. 68)

In a small skillet, sauté onion and garlic in Sunlite Oil until onions are transparent; set aside. In a bowl, combine milk, eggs, biscuit mix and seasonings. Fold in zucchini, cheese, garlic and onion. Turn mixture into pie shell and bake at 350°F 40 to 45 minutes, or until lightly browned and slightly set. Serve warm or at room temperature. Serves 6 to 8.

zucchini chips *(illustrated page 4)*

Perfect first course or side dish

		Sunlite Oil
125 ml	½	cup flour
5 ml	1	teasp. seasoned salt
5 ml	1	teasp. garlic powder
3 ml	½	teasp. pepper
	3	medium zucchini, diagonally sliced
	2	eggs, beaten
250 ml	1	cup fine, dry bread crumbs
		Grated Parmesan cheese

Fill a Dutch oven or heavy kettle ⅓ full with Sunlite Oil. Heat to 350°F and maintain temperature with deep-fry thermometer. Meanwhile, in plastic bag, combine flour, seasoned salt, garlic powder and pepper. Add zucchini slices; shake to coat. Dip in egg and then in bread crumbs. Fry, a few slices at a time, in hot oil 40 to 60 seconds. Sprinkle with Parmesan. Makes 4 servings.

soy nuts

Nutritious munching

450 g	1	lb. dried soybeans
		Boiling water
125 ml	½	cup Sunlite Oil
		Salt or seasoned salt

Soak soybeans in a bowl overnight in enough water to cover by 3 inches. Skim off foam and hulls that float to surface; drain well. Spread soybeans on flat surface to dry. Heat ¼ *cup* Sunlite Oil in skillet over medium heat. Add *half* the soybeans; sauté 15 to 20 minutes or until golden brown and crunchy. Stir frequently. Remove; spread on paper towels. *Repeat* with *remaining* soybeans and Sunlite Oil. Season with salt. Store in plastic bag or tightly covered jar. Makes 6 cups.

marinated mushrooms

Wonderfully hot and spicy

375 ml	1½	cups Sunlite Italian Dressing (p. 14)
56 g	1	(2-oz.) can marinated jalapeno peppers, chopped
675 g	1½	lbs. mushrooms, washed, stems removed

In a large saucepan, bring Sunlite Italian Dressing and jalapeno peppers to a boil. Add mushrooms, *lower* heat; simmer 2 minutes; cool. Pour into glass jar or casserole. Cover; marinate overnight or up to three days for maximum flavor. Makes 6 servings.

fondue

Leave the cooking to your guests

225 g	½	lb. top beef sirloin
225 g	½	lb. boneless chicken breast
225 g	½	lb. large mushrooms, halved
	2	zucchini, cut in thick slices
		Sunlite Oil
		Bamboo skewers or fondue forks
		Savory Dressing for dip (p. 15)
		Curry Dressing for dip (p. 15)

Trim fat from sirloin; cut into bite-size cubes. Remove skin from chicken; cut into bite-size pieces. Arrange on serving platter with mushroom halves and zucchini slices. Fill a heavy saucepan or fondue pot ⅓ full with Sunlite Oil. Heat to 375°F and maintain temperature with a deep-fry thermometer. Allow guests to spear cubes of meat, chicken and vegetables on skewers or fondue forks; immerse in hot oil 30 seconds to 1 minute to desired doneness. Serve dips in small bowls. Makes 4 to 6 servings.

antipasto nibblers *(illustrated page 4)*

Snack on these while watching TV

1 bunch radishes	1 small cucumber
2 small zucchini	4 ribs celery
1 small head cauliflower	1 green pepper
4 carrots	7 small leaves red cabbage

Ranch Style Dressing (recipe below)

Wash and trim vegetables; leave radishes whole, slice zucchini, separate cauliflower into small flowerettes and cut remaining vegetables in julienne strips. Arrange separately on cabbage leaves on a large serving tray. Serve Ranch Style Dressing as dip for vegetables. Serves 10 to 12.

ranch style dressing

250 ml	1	cup Sunlite Mayonnaise (p. 15)
180 ml	¾	cup sour cream
125 ml	½	cup milk
15 ml	1	Tablesp. dry parsley flakes
10 ml	2	teasp. instant minced onions
1 ml	¼	teasp. garlic powder
1 ml	¼	teasp. onion powder
3 ml	½	teasp. salt

Combine all ingredients in a small bowl; mix thoroughly. Store in a covered nonmetal container in refrigerator. Makes 1 pint.

superb salads and dressings

Light refreshers—for any occasion

classic caesar salad (illustrated opposite)

Tradition speaks for itself

	1 clove garlic, cut
	½ head Romaine lettuce
125 ml	½ cup croutons
60 ml	¼ cup grated Parmesan cheese
	4 to 6 anchovy fillets, chopped
125 ml	½ cup Sunlite Vinaigrette Dressing made with lemon juice (p. 14)
	1 egg, slightly beaten

Rub a bowl with cut side of garlic clove; discard garlic. Wash lettuce; dry on paper towels; tear in bite-size pieces into seasoned bowl. Add croutons, Parmesan cheese and anchovies. Just before serving, add Sunlite Vinaigrette Dressing; toss lightly; add egg; toss again. Makes 4 servings.

carrot-raisin salad

Vegetable and salad in one

500 ml	2 cups peeled, shredded carrots
125 ml	½ cup raisins
60 ml	¼ cup crushed pineapple
125 ml	½ cup Sunlite Mayonnaise (p. 15)
	4 lettuce-leaf "cups"

In a bowl, combine all ingredients *except* lettuce; toss to mix. Chill. Serve on lettuce leaves. Makes 4 servings.

shrimp salad special

Lightly dressed and seasoned

	½ head iceberg lettuce
225 g	8 ozs. frozen cooked shrimp, thawed and drained
	1 hard cooked egg, sliced
64 g	1 (2¼-oz.) can sliced ripe olives, drained
	1 tomato, sliced into wedges
60 ml	¼ cup cubed Monterey Jack cheese
60 ml	¼ cup Sunlite Oil
30 ml	2 Tablesp. lemon juice
15 ml	1 Tablesp. red wine vinegar
15 ml	1 Tablesp. sugar
8 ml	1½ teasp. seasoned salt
5 ml	1 teasp. dill weed

Wash lettuce; dry on paper towels; tear in bite-size pieces into bowl. Add shrimp, hard cooked eggs, olives, tomato and cheese. Toss to mix; chill. Combine Sunlite Oil with remaining ingredients, shake well in covered jar. Just before serving, pour over chilled shrimp salad ingredients; toss lightly. Makes 4 servings.

sunlite vinaigrette dressing

Light and sparkling oil dressing

125 ml	½ cup Sunlite Oil
60 ml	¼ cup cider vinegar or as variation directs
5 ml	1 teasp. salt
1 ml	¼ teasp. pepper

Combine all ingredients in covered jar; shake well. Shake each time before using. Makes ¾ cup.

FLAVOR VARIATIONS:	¾ CUP VINAIGRETTE PLUS:	ESPECIALLY GOOD ON:
BLEU CHEESE	3 Tablesp. crumbled bleu cheese	Head Lettuce or Mixed Green Salads
CHUTNEY	¼ cup chopped chutney 2 Tablesp. ketchup 1½ Tablesp. Worcestershire 1 Tablesp. lemon juice 1 teasp. sugar	Seafood, Meat and Fruit Salads or Marinade/Baste for Chicken
CREAMY	¼ cup sour cream 2 Tablesp. bacon bits ¼ teasp. minced parsley	Seafood, Meat, Spinach or Vegetable Salads
EXOTIC HERB	1 Tablesp. minced parsley 1 teasp. thyme ¼ teasp. each: basil, rosemary and oregano	Mixed Green Salad or Marinade/Baste for Beef and Fish
FRENCH	¼ cup wine vinegar instead ⅓ cup ketchup 2 Tablesp. sugar 1 teasp. minced onion ¾ teasp. seasoned salt	Head Lettuce, Mixed Green, Vegetable Salads or Marinade/Baste for Beef or Chicken
HORSERADISH	1 Tablesp. prepared horseradish	Beef or Mixed Vegetable Salads
ITALIAN	¼ cup lemon juice instead ¼ teasp. Italian seasoning ¼ teasp. garlic powder	Mixed Green, Antipasto Vegetables, Tomato Salads
SUPREME	¼ cup orange marmalade 1 teasp. paprika ½ teasp. seasoned salt ½ teasp. celery seed	Fruit, Citrus with Greens or Marinade/Baste for Chicken and Pork

14

sunlite mayonnaise

Homemade fresh in minutes

	1 egg
1 ml	¼ teasp. salt
30 ml	2 Tablesp. lemon juice
250 ml	1 cup Sunlite Oil

Have all ingredients at room temperature. Combine egg, salt, lemon juice and ¼ *cup* Sunlite Oil in blender container. Blend together until mixture begins to thicken. Blend in *remaining* ¾ *cup* Sunlite Oil, pouring in a thin stream, until mixture is thick and smooth, about 2 minutes. Allow slightly longer beating time for rotary or electric beater. Makes 1 cup.

FLAVOR VARIATIONS:	1 CUP MAYONNAISE PLUS:	ESPECIALLY GOOD ON:
CURRY	½ cup sour cream 2 Tablesp. lemon juice ½ teasp. curry powder ¼ teasp. seasoned salt	Seafood, Chicken, Rice and Vegetable Salads *or* as a Dip
GUACAMOLE	1 cup mashed avocado 1½ Tablesp. diced canned green chilies ½ teasp. seasoned salt ¼ teasp. Tabasco ¼ teasp. garlic powder	Vegetable, Shredded Lettuce, Seafood Salads *or* as a Dip
SAVORY	1½ teasp. seasoned salt 1 teasp. dill weed ½ teasp. Worcestershire ½ teasp. paprika ½ teasp. pepper	Meat, Mixed Green Salads *or* as a Dip
TARTAR SAUCE	¼ cup minced celery ¼ cup minced onion 2 Tablesp. pickle relish 1 Tablesp. lemon juice	Broiled, Fried *or* Baked Seafood
THOUSAND ISLAND	½ cup ketchup ¼ cup pickle relish	Seafood, Head Lettuce and Mixed Green Salads
VELVET	1 8-oz. carton yogurt 1 teasp. sugar	Fruit Salads

chicken salad

Excellent sandwich filling too

500 ml	2	cups cubed cooked chicken
125 ml	½	cup sliced celery
60 ml	¼	cup diced green onion
	1	hard cooked egg, chopped
125 ml	½	cup Sunlite Mayonnaise (p. 15)
3 ml	½	teasp. seasoned salt
3 ml	½	teasp. sugar
3 ml	½	teasp. Italian seasoning
1 ml	¼	teasp. garlic powder
1 ml	¼	teasp. pepper

In a medium bowl, combine all ingredients; blend well. Chill thoroughly. Serve on lettuce garnished with wedges of tomato, if desired. Makes 4 servings.

california potato salad

30 ml	2	Tablesp. cider vinegar
10 ml	2	teasp. sugar
5 ml	1	teasp. seasoned salt
3 ml	½	teasp. pepper
	4 to 5	medium potatoes, cooked and diced
125 ml	½	cup Sunlite Mayonnaise (p. 15)
3 ml	½	teasp. prepared mustard
.5 ml	⅛	teasp. curry powder (optional)
	2	hard cooked eggs, chopped
60 ml	¼	cup minced onion

In a large bowl, combine vinegar, sugar and spices; add potatoes; toss to mix thoroughly. Refrigerate, covered, 1 hour; stir once or twice. Meanwhile, in a small bowl, combine Sunlite Mayonnaise, mustard and curry; add to potatoes along with remaining ingredients. Toss lightly to mix. Makes 4 servings.

crisp and creamy coleslaw

250 ml	1	cup Sunlite Mayonnaise (p. 15)
30 ml	2	Tablesp. grated carrots or red cabbage
30 ml	2	Tablesp. white vinegar
5 ml	1	teasp. sugar
3 ml	½	teasp. salt
	1	medium head cabbage, shredded

In a medium bowl, combine all ingredients *except* cabbage; mix thoroughly. Add cabbage; mix. Chill. Makes 8 to 10 servings.

greek salad

	1	large head Romaine lettuce
225 g	8	ozs. Feta cheese *or* Monterey Jack cheese *or* crumbled cottage cheese
64 g	1	(2¼-oz.) can ripe olives, sliced
	6	radishes, sliced thinly
	1	cucumber, sliced
	1	tomato, cut in wedges
180 ml	¾	cup Sunlite Vinaigrette Dressing (p. 14)
3 ml	½	teasp. oregano

Wash lettuce; pat dry on paper towels; tear in bite-size pieces into a bowl. Add cheese, olives and vegetables. Toss to mix; refrigerate. Meanwhile, prepare Sunlite Vinaigrette Dressing, add oregano and shake well in covered jar. Add to chilled salad ingredients just before serving; toss lightly to mix.
Makes 6 to 8 servings.

Feta is a Greek semisoft cheese made from sheep's milk; Monterey Jack from the United States, Muenster from Germany and Fontina from Italy can be substituted.

spinach salad supreme

	1	bunch fresh spinach
	1	orange, peeled and sliced
	½	avocado, sliced in crescents
60 ml	¼	cup julienne strips Swiss cheese
	½	small red onion, sliced and separated into rings
	4	pitted prunes, cut in half
1 ml	¼	teasp. curry powder
1 ml	¼	teasp. dried parsley flakes
125 ml	½	cup Sunlite Italian Dressing (p. 14)
		Walnut halves (optional)

Wash spinach; pat dry on paper towels; tear in bite-size pieces into bowl. Add orange, avocado, cheese, onion and prunes. Toss to mix; refrigerate. Meanwhile, add curry and parsley to Sunlite Italian Dressing; mix thoroughly. Toss with chilled salad ingredients just before serving. Garnish with walnuts, if desired. Makes 4 servings.

gelatin party layers *(illustrated opposite)*

Creamy nut filling

170 g	1	(6-oz.) pkg. strawberry-flavored gelatin
	2	large bananas, sliced
225 g	1	(8-oz.) pkg. cream cheese, softened
170 ml	⅔	cup Sunlite Mayonnaise (p. 15)
125 ml	½	cup chopped walnuts
170 g	1	(6-oz.) carton non-dairy whipped topping

In a bowl, prepare gelatin with water according to package directions; pour *half* into 2½-quart glass casserole; stir in bananas; chill until set. Chill *remaining* gelatin until it *starts to set.* Meanwhile, in a medium bowl, blend cream cheese, Sunlite Mayonnaise and walnuts; spread evenly over *firm* layer of gelatin in casserole. Blend whipped topping into *partially set* gelatin until smooth and creamy; spoon over cream cheese layer. Chill until set. Garnish with additional whipped topping, strawberries and mint leaves if desired. Makes 8 servings.

seashell supper salad

Wonderful pot luck take-along

750 ml	3	cups cooked shell macaroni, chilled
200 g	1	(7-oz.) can tuna packed in water, drained
	2	hard cooked eggs, chopped
125 ml	½	cup each: diced green pepper and celery
60 ml	¼	cup minced onion
60 ml	¼	cup chopped sweet pickle
5 ml	1	teasp. seasoned salt
3 ml	½	teasp. paprika
.5 ml	⅛	teasp. pepper
125 ml	½	cup Sunlite Mayonnaise (p. 15)
		Lettuce leaves and tomato wedges

In a bowl, combine macaroni, tuna, hard cooked eggs, vegetables, pickle and seasonings; toss to mix thoroughly. Refrigerate. Add Sunlite Mayonnaise when ready to serve; mix gently. Serve on lettuce leaves; garnish with tomato wedges. Makes 4 to 6 servings.

dilled cucumber

	4	tomatoes, pulp removed and chopped
	1	small unpeeled cucumber, diced
3 ml	½	teasp. dill weed
125 ml	½	cup Sunlite Creamy Dressing (p. 14)

Combine tomatoes, cucumber, dill weed and ¼ *cup* Sunlite Creamy Dressing; chill. Fill tomato cups, top with *remaining* dressing. Makes 4 servings.

gingered fruit salad *(illustrated page 19)*

Perfect dressing for any seasonal fruit

225 g	1 (8-oz.) carton peach yogurt
125 ml	½ cup Sunlite Mayonnaise (p. 15)
1 ml	¼ teasp. ground ginger
	1 medium pineapple
	1 pink grapefruit, sectioned
	1 pint strawberries, washed and hulled
	½ honeydew melon, cut into 1-inch cubes

Combine yogurt, Sunlite Mayonnaise, and ginger in a small bowl; refrigerate. Slice pineapple in half lengthwise, leaving crown intact. Scoop out pineapple leaving ½-inch-thick shells. Cut pineapple meat into 1-inch chunks, discarding core. Combine pineapple chunks and *remaining* fruits; arrange in pineapple halves. Serve with chilled ginger dressing. Makes 8 servings.

Cut around pineapple, leaving ½-inch shell

Scoop out pineapple; cut out core and discard

Cut pineapple in chunks; return to shell with fruit

oriental tempter

Top with sesame seeds

	½ head Romaine or iceberg lettuce
110 g	¼ lb. fresh bean sprouts
312 g	1 (11-oz.) can Mandarin oranges, drained
60 ml	¼ cup sliced water chestnuts
125 ml	½ cup Sunlite Vinaigrette Dressing (p. 14)
22 ml	1½ Tablesp. brown sugar
15 ml	1 Tablesp. soy sauce
250 ml	1 cup chow mein noodles

Wash lettuce; pat dry on paper towels; tear in bite-size pieces into bowl. Add bean sprouts, orange sections and water chestnuts. Toss to mix; refrigerate, covered. Meanwhile, combine *remaining* ingredients and shake well in a covered jar. Pour over chilled salad ingredients just before serving; toss lightly. Top with noodles. Makes 4 servings.

beef vinaigrette salad bowl

Meal-size for man-size appetites

500 ml	2 cups diced cooked beef
500 ml	2 cups diced cooked potatoes
125 ml	½ cup chopped green pepper
125 ml	½ cup chopped celery
60 ml	¼ cup minced onion
30 ml	2 Tablesp. chopped pimiento
	¾ cup Sunlite Horseradish Dressing (p. 14)
	Boston lettuce
60 ml	¼ cup minced fresh parsley

Combine first 6 ingredients in a large bowl; mix gently. Pour Sunlite Horseradish Dressing over all; chill 1 to 2 hours. Stir once or twice. Line salad serving bowl with lettuce leaves. Fill center with beef vinaigrette mixture. Sprinkle with parsley. Makes 4 to 6 servings.

mexicali toss

Fabulous main-dish salad

450 g	1 lb. ground beef
35 g	1 (1¼-oz.) packet taco seasoning mix
180 ml	¾ cup water
	½ head iceberg lettuce, shredded
	1 tomato, diced
3 ml	½ cup sliced green onions
1 ml	¼ teasp. crushed red pepper
60 ml	¼ cup Sunlite Vinaigrette Dressing (p. 14)
	1 recipe tortilla chips (p. 6) *or* (10-oz.) bag
250 ml	1 cup shredded Cheddar cheese
	1 recipe Guacamole (p. 15)

In a skillet, brown ground beef until it loses redness; drain fat. Stir in seasoning mix and water. Bring to boil; *reduce heat* and simmer, uncovered, 15 minutes, stirring occasionally. Meanwhile, in a bowl, toss lettuce, tomatoes, green onions and red peppers with Sunlite Vinaigrette Dressing. To assemble, arrange layer of tortilla chips on 4 serving plates; spoon equal portions of meat mixture and cheese on each; top with equal portions of salad and generous dollops of Guacamole. Makes 4 servings.

For Tostadas, use a crisply fried corn tortilla as the base. Spread with heated refried beans; top with meat mixture, salad, cheese and sour cream.

marvelous meats
& side dishes

Entrées and other dishes that make the meal

spicy barbecued spareribs *(illustrated opposite)*

A western favorite everywhere

5000 g	2	strips (about 5½ to 6 lbs.) pork spareribs
		Seasoned salt
250 ml	1	cup minced onion
	2	large cloves garlic, minced
45 ml	3	Tablesp. Sunlite Oil
225 g	1	(8-oz.) can tomato sauce
125 ml	½	cup <u>each</u>: ketchup and wine vinegar
85 ml	⅓	cup lemon juice
60 ml	¼	cup Worcestershire
60 ml	¼	cup brown sugar, packed
20 ml	4	teasp. chili powder
10 ml	2	teasp. celery seed
5 ml	1	teasp. ground cumin

Sprinkle ribs with seasoned salt. Place on hot grill about 5 inches from coals or source of heat. Cook 45 minutes to 1 hour; turn frequently. Meanwhile, in a small pan, sauté onion and garlic in Sunlite Oil until onion is transparent. Add *remaining* ingredients. Heat to boiling. *Reduce heat;* simmer, uncovered, 25 to 30 minutes. Use to baste spareribs last 10 to 15 minutes of grilling; turn and baste often. Makes 10 to 12 servings.

Oven Baked: Place on rack in shallow baking pan. Bake at 375°F 45 minutes to 1 hour. Remove from rack; drain excess fat. Return ribs to pan; pour sauce over ribs. Bake 20 minutes longer.

indian summer stir-fry

Quick cooked for garden fresh flavor

	3	carrots, thinly sliced
	3	medium zucchini, cut in ¼-inch slices
	1	small onion, sliced, separated into rings
	1	small green pepper, cut in ½-inch squares
250 ml	1	cup fresh or frozen corn
125 ml	½	cup sliced celery
	4	large mushrooms, sliced
60 ml	¼	cup Sunlite Oil
3 ml	½	teasp. salt
3 ml	½	teasp. basil

Prepare vegetables; keep separate from each other. Heat Sunlite Oil in a wok, electric or regular skillet over medium heat. Add carrots, zucchini and onion rings; stir to mix. Cook, *covered,* 3 minutes; stir once. Stir in green pepper, corn and celery; stir and fry *uncovered* 3 to 5 minutes. Stir in mushrooms, salt and basil; stir and fry about 2 to 3 minutes longer. Do not overcook. Makes 4 servings.

veal marsala

As impressive as it is delicious

900 g	2	lbs. veal scallops
	2	eggs, separated
30 ml	2	Tablesp. water
250 ml	1	cup fine, dry bread crumbs
3 ml	½	teasp. basil, crushed
		Dash garlic powder
		Flour for dredging
85 ml	⅓	cup Sunlite Oil
375 ml	1½	cups sliced mushrooms
		Salt and pepper
250 ml	1	cup beef broth
125 ml	½	cup Marsala wine
		Parsley, chopped

Pound scallops to ⅛-inch thickness. Cut into 3 × 4-inch pieces. Beat egg *whites* and water in one small dish; combine bread crumbs, basil and garlic powder in another. Dip scallops in crumbs, then egg, then flour. Chill several hours. Sauté scallops, a few at a time, in Sunlite Oil in a large skillet until golden. Keep warm. In same skillet, sauté mushrooms until tender; season with salt and pepper. Pour over scallops. Bring broth to boil in skillet. Beat egg *yolks* with Marsala wine. Beat in several spoonfuls of broth to yolk mixture; return to skillet, stirring constantly. Cook and stir over low heat, until sauce thickens. Do not boil. Spoon over scallops and mushrooms. Sprinkle with parsley; serve at once. Makes 6 to 8 servings.

Coat and chill scallops ahead of time. Dipping scallops in flour *after* applying crumb coating helps keep them from sticking to the pan during cooking.

glazed sesame carrots

A touch of sweetness for an old standby

450 g	1	lb. small carrots, cut in 2-inch strips
30 ml	2	Tablesp. Sunlite Oil
60 ml	¼	cup water
45 ml	3	Tablesp. brown sugar
15 ml	1	Tablesp. sesame seeds
1 ml	¼	teasp. salt

Sauté carrots in Sunlite Oil in a small skillet over medium heat until lightly browned. Stir in remaining ingredients. Cover; cook over low heat 8 to 10 minutes until just tender. Stir once or twice. Makes 4 servings.

garden harvest beef stew

One-dish favorite summer or winter

450 g	1	lb. lean beef stew meat, cut in 1-inch cubes
60 ml	¼	cup Sunlite Oil
250 ml	1	cup chopped onion
	1	clove garlic, minced
500 ml	2	cups water
	2	beef bouillon cubes
5 ml	1	teasp. salt
3 ml	½	teasp. basil, crushed
1 ml	¼	teasp. pepper
	1	bay leaf
	2	carrots, cut in ¼-inch slices
	2	ribs celery, sliced ¼-inch thick
	2	medium zucchini, cut in ½-inch pieces
250 ml	1	cup fresh or frozen whole kernel corn
250 ml	1	cup fresh or frozen cut green beans
	1	large tomato, coarsely chopped
30 ml	2	Tablesp. quick-cooking tapioca

In a Dutch oven or large saucepan, brown beef in Sunlite Oil. Add onion and garlic; cook until tender. Stir in water, bouillon cubes and seasonings. Bring to a boil. Simmer, covered, 1½ to 2 hours, until meat is almost tender. Add vegetables and tapioca. Simmer, covered, 40 minutes longer or until meat and vegetables are tender. Makes 4 to 6 servings.

oven roasted potatoes

Easy-to-do crispy potatoes

	3	medium potatoes, pared and quartered or cut in ½-inch-thick slices
45 ml	3	Tablesp. Sunlite Oil
45 ml	3	Tablesp. fine, dry bread crumbs
45 ml	3	Tablesp. grated Parmesan cheese
		Salt and pepper

Dip potatoes in Sunlite Oil, then in bread crumbs mixed with Parmesan. Arrange in single layer in shallow baking dish. Bake at 375°F 40 to 45 minutes for quarters (30 to 35 minutes for slices) until tender and nicely browned. Sprinkle with salt and pepper. Makes 4 to 6 servings.

broiled stuffed pork chops

Quick and easy for a special meal

125 ml	½ cup chopped celery
125 ml	½ cup minced onion
125 ml	½ cup shredded carrot
	Sunlite Oil
250 ml	1 cup warm water
170 ml	⅔ cup quick-cooking brown rice
15 ml	1 Tablesp. chopped parsley
5 ml	1 teasp. seasoned salt
1 ml	¼ teasp. thyme, crushed
	4 (1-inch-thick) pork chops, with pocket
	Salt, pepper and paprika

In a small saucepan, sauté celery, onion and carrots in *2 tablespoons* Sunlite Oil 3 minutes. Add water, rice, parsley, seasoned salt and thyme. Bring to a boil; *reduce* heat; simmer, covered, 10 to 15 minutes or until tender. Spoon an equal amount of stuffing into each pork chop pocket; close opening with toothpicks. Brush both sides of chops lightly with oil; sprinkle with salt, pepper and paprika. Arrange on cold broiler pan. Broil 2 to 3 inches from heat, 8 to 10 minutes *on each side*. Remove toothpicks. Makes 4 servings.

french fried potatoes

Sunlite Oil is the secret

900 g	5 to 6 medium baking potatoes or 1 (32-oz.) pkg. frozen French fries
	Sunlite Oil
	Salt and pepper

Wash and pare potatoes; cut into ½-inch-thick lengthwise strips; cover with ice water. Fill deep-fry kettle ⅓ full with Sunlite Oil, or pour Sunlite Oil ½ inch deep in a large skillet to shallow-fry. Heat to 375°F and maintain temperature with deep-fry thermometer. Drain potatoes and pat dry. Fry only as many potatoes at a time as oil will cover. Lower potatoes slowly into oil using a frying basket or slotted spoon. Fry about 6 to 7 minutes until golden brown. Drain on paper towel; keep warm in oven at low heat. Sprinkle with salt and pepper to serve. Makes 4 to 6 servings.

Potatoes high in starch and low in sugar content like Russet or Kennebec are best for deep-frying. They don't brown too quickly.

neapolitan beef pie

Appetizing layers in a marvelous crust

340 g	¾	lb. ground beef
	1	small onion, finely chopped
	1	to 2 cloves garlic, crushed
170 g	1	(6-oz.) can tomato paste
180 ml	¾	cup water
30 ml	2	Tablesp. Worcestershire
5 ml	1	teasp. Italian seasoning
5 ml	1	teasp. seasoned salt
5 ml	1	teasp. brown sugar
250 ml	1	cup small curd cottage cheese
	1	egg, slightly beaten
284 g	1	(10-oz.) pkg. frozen chopped spinach, thawed and pressed dry
		Cheddar Cheese Crust (recipe below)
60 ml	¼	cup grated Parmesan cheese

Sauté ground beef, onion and garlic in a 10-inch skillet until beef loses redness; drain fat. Add tomato paste, water, Worcestershire, Italian seasoning, seasoned salt and brown sugar; simmer 5 minutes. Meanwhile, in a small bowl, blend cottage cheese and egg. Pat spinach into bottom of Cheddar Cheese Crust. Spoon on cottage cheese mixture in a layer, then meat sauce over all; sprinkle with Parmesan cheese. Bake at 375°F 20 to 25 minutes. Let stand 5 to 10 minutes before serving. Makes 6 servings.

cheddar cheese crust

Delicious for open-face apple pie

335 ml	1⅓	cups sifted all-purpose flour
125 ml	½	cup shredded Cheddar cheese
3 ml	½	teasp. seasoned salt
85 ml	⅓	cup Sunlite Oil
45 ml	3	Tablesp. cold milk

In a bowl, mix flour, cheese and salt. Pour Sunlite Oil and milk, all at once, into flour mixture. Stir just until mixed. Press into smooth ball, flatten slightly. Place between 2 sheets of wax paper 12 inches square. Dampen table top to prevent slipping. Roll out gently to edges of paper. Peel off top paper. If dough tears, mend without moistening. Place paper-side-up in a 9-inch pie pan. Peel off paper. Ease and fit pastry into pan. Trim and flute edge; prick thoroughly with fork. Bake at 475°F 7 to 9 minutes until golden. Cool. Makes 1 (9-inch) pie shell.

flank steak teriyaki

Marinate overnight to enhance the flavor

125 ml	½ cup soy sauce
85 ml	⅓ cup Sunlite Oil
60 ml	¼ cup honey
30 ml	2 Tablesp. red wine vinegar
	1 clove garlic, minced
5 ml	1 teasp. ground ginger
1350 g	2 to 3 lbs. flank steak (about 2)

In a small bowl or jar with tight-fitting lid, combine all ingredients *except* steak; mix well. Score flank steak on both sides. Place in glass baking dish(es); pour teriyaki marinade over all. Refrigerate 3 to 24 hours; turn once. Broil steak 6 inches from heat, about 5 minutes on each side to desired doneness; baste occasionally with marinade. To serve, slice thinly across grain. Makes 6 to 8 servings.

perfect onion rings *(illustrated page 22)*

Tempura-style or crusty-breaded

	3 to 4 sweet Bermuda onions
180 ml	¾ cup flour
180 ml	¾ cup milk
	1 egg
3 ml	½ teasp. sugar
3 ml	½ teasp. salt
	Fine, dry bread crumbs* (optional)
	Sunlite Oil

Peel and cut onions into ¼-inch-thick slices; separate into rings; refrigerate, covered. In a small bowl with beater or in blender, combine flour, milk, egg, sugar and salt; beat until smooth. Fill deep-fry pan or large deep skillet ⅓ full with Sunlite Oil. Heat to 375°F and maintain temperature with deep-fry thermometer. Dip onion rings, 5 or 6 at a time, into batter with a fork; hold over bowl to drain excess*. Lower gently into hot oil and fry 2 to 3 minutes until golden. Drain on paper towel; keep warm in low oven until frying is completed. Makes 4 to 6 servings.

*If crustier onion rings are desired, dip batter-coated onion rings in fine dry bread crumbs before frying.

sweet and sour pork

Serve over hot cooked rice

	2	eggs, well beaten
90 ml	6	Tablesp. all-purpose flour
30 ml	2	Tablesp. milk
5 ml	1	teasp. salt
675 g	1½	lbs. boneless pork
750 ml	3	cups Sunlite Oil
60 ml	¼	cup brown sugar, packed
30 ml	2	Tablesp. cornstarch
225 g	1	(8-oz.) can tomato sauce
60 ml	¼	cup cider vinegar
60 ml	¼	cup light corn syrup
560 g	1	(20-oz.) can pineapple chunks, drained *reserving* ½ cup juice
1 ml	¼	teasp. garlic salt
.5 ml	⅛	teasp. pepper
	1	green pepper, cut in 1-inch squares
	¼	onion, sliced in thin strips

In a medium bowl, mix eggs, flour, milk and salt until smooth. Add pork cut in 1-inch cubes; stir to coat. In a 12-inch skillet, heat Sunlite Oil to 375°F. Using a slotted spoon to allow excess batter to drain off, add *half* the pork; fry about 10 minutes until golden and tender. Drain on paper towels. Repeat. Meanwhile, combine brown sugar and cornstarch in a saucepan. Add tomato sauce, vinegar, corn syrup, *reserved* pineapple juice, garlic salt and pepper. Cook and stir until thickened; add green pepper, pineapple chunks, onion and fried pork. Simmer 10 minutes, covered. Makes 6 servings.

---

julienne beans almondine

Crisp-tender and quick

450 g	1	lb. green beans
125 ml	½	cup chopped onion
30 ml	2	Tablesp. Sunlite Oil
60 ml	¼	cup water
3 ml	½	teasp. salt
45 ml	3	Tablesp. toasted slivered almonds*

Wash beans; remove stem ends and cut in thin julienne-style strips. In 1½-quart saucepan, sauté onion in Sunlite Oil until transparent. Add beans, water and salt; mix gently. Simmer, covered, 15 minutes until crisp-tender; stir occasionally. Sprinkle with almonds. Makes 4 servings.

*Toss almonds with 2 to 3 drops Sunlite Oil; "toast" in small skillet over low heat, stirring constantly, until golden.

fettucini american style *(illustrated opposite)*

Noodles never tasted so good

225 g	8 ozs. fettucini
60 ml	¼ cup margarine, softened
125 ml	½ cup grated Parmesan cheese
180 ml	¾ cup hot milk
60 ml	¼ cup Sunlite Oil
375 ml	1½ cups fresh vegetables: thinly sliced carrots, mushrooms and zucchini, cut green beans, asparagus tips and peas
3 ml	½ teasp. salt

In 1½-quart saucepan, cook noodles as package directs for 6 minutes. Drain thoroughly; place in a warm bowl. Add margarine and Parmesan cheese. Toss lightly about 1 minute using a fork and spoon until noodles are well coated. Add hot milk and Sunlite Oil; continue tossing gently until well mixed and a creamy sauce is formed. Meanwhile, steam vegetables until just crisp-tender. Stir hot vegetables and salt into noodle mixture. Serve at once. Makes 4 to 6 servings.

In place of fresh vegetables, add 1 (10-oz.) package frozen mixed vegetables, cooked and drained according to package directions.

broiled tomatoes

A handsome and tasty serve-along dish

125 ml	½ cup dry, coarse bread crumbs
15 ml	1 Tablesp. grated Parmesan cheese
30 ml	2 Tablesp. Sunlite Oil
3 ml	½ teasp. seasoned salt
3 ml	½ teasp. finely minced onion
	4 medium tomatoes, firm but ripe

Combine all ingredients *except* tomatoes in a small bowl; mix well; set aside. Wash tomatoes; remove stem ends and cut in half crosswise. Place on a shallow pan cut-side up. Spread cut surface of each with crumb mixture. Broil, 5 to 6 inches from heat, about 10 minutes until golden brown. Makes 6 to 8 servings.

steak diane

A "flamed" dish to make you famous

675 g	1½	lbs. boneless top beef sirloin, ½ inch thick, cut in 6 servings
		Salt
3 ml	½	teasp. coarse ground pepper
8 ml	1½	teasp. dry mustard
60 ml	¼	cup Sunlite Oil
250 ml	1	cup sliced mushrooms
45 ml	3	Tablesp. fresh lemon juice
15 ml	1	Tablesp. minced chives
10 ml	2	teasp. Worcestershire
60 ml	¼	cup brandy (optional)

With meat mallet, pound steak to ⅓-inch thickness. Sprinkle *each* side with salt. Blend pepper and mustard; pound into both sides of meat. In a skillet or blazer pan of chafing dish, heat Sunlite Oil to sizzling. Add 3 steaks; sauté 2 minutes on each side or to desired doneness. Transfer to hot serving plate; keep warm. Sauté *remaining* steaks; remove; keep warm. In same pan, sauté mushrooms in drippings until tender. With a slotted spoon, place mushrooms over steaks. Add lemon juice, chives and Worcestershire to drippings; bring to a boil. To "flame," heat brandy to lukewarm in saucepan; flame and add to skillet. When flames subside, pour sauce over steaks. Serve immediately. Makes 6 servings.

stuffed mushrooms

Succulent bites of impressive tenderness

450 g	16	large mushrooms (about 1 lb.)
		Sunlite Oil
60 ml	¼	cup minced onion
60 ml	¼	cup finely shredded carrot
250 ml	1	cup cornbread stuffing mix
3 ml	½	teasp. rosemary
85 ml	⅓	cup hot water

Wash mushrooms; pat dry. Remove stems; chop coarsely; reserve. Brush mushroom *caps* lightly with Sunlite Oil; arrange cap-side down in a shallow 2-quart baking dish. Meanwhile, in a saucepan, sauté mushroom stems, onion and carrot in *1 tablespoon* Sunlite Oil until onion is soft. Add stuffing mix and rosemary; moisten with hot water; mix thoroughly. Spoon into mushroom caps. Bake, covered, at 375°F about 15 minutes. Remove cover; bake 5 minutes longer. Makes 4 servings or 16 appetizers.

deep dish mexi-pizza

South of the border flavor twist

450 g	1	lb. ground beef
	1	onion, chopped
440 g	1	(15½-oz.) can kidney beans, undrained
425 g	1	(15-oz.) can tomato sauce
10 ml	2	teasp. chili powder
		Salt
3 ml	½	teasp. ground cumin
375 ml	1½	cups sifted all-purpose flour
125 ml	½	cup cornmeal
15 ml	1	Tablesp. baking powder
85 ml	⅓	cup Sunlite Oil
170 ml	⅔	cup cold milk
375 ml	1½	cups shredded Cheddar or Monterey Jack cheese
		Toppings*

In a large saucepan, cook ground beef and onion until beef loses redness; drain fat. Stir in kidney beans, tomato sauce, chili powder, *1 teaspoon* salt and ground cumin; simmer, covered, 10 minutes. Meanwhile, in a bowl, combine flour, cornmeal, baking powder and *1 teaspoon* salt. Add Sunlite Oil and milk. Stir with a fork until mixture forms a ball. Pat evenly into a lightly oiled 9 × 13-inch baking pan forming an edge about ¾ inch high. Spread meat mixture evenly over crust. Sprinkle with cheese. Bake at 425°F 20 minutes. Top as desired. Cut in rectangles. Makes 6 servings.

*Suggested Toppings: Bottled hot sauce (optional), avocado wedges, chopped tomatoes, diced green chilies, guacamole, shredded lettuce, sliced ripe olives, sour cream.

risotto

Crunchy good and packed with nutrition

	1	small onion, chopped
250 ml	1	cup quick-cooking brown rice
30 ml	2	Tablesp. Sunlite Oil
305 g	1	(10¾-oz.) can chicken broth
250 ml	1	cup water
5 ml	1	teasp. salt
125 ml	½	cup frozen peas
125 ml	½	cup chopped salted peanuts
.5 ml	⅛	teasp. pepper

In a 1-quart saucepan, sauté onion and rice in Sunlite Oil until onion is transparent. Add chicken broth, water and salt. Bring to a boil; lower heat and simmer, covered, 10 minutes until rice is almost tender. Stir in peas, peanuts and pepper. Cook, covered, about 5 minutes longer. Makes 4 servings.

herbed leg of lamb

A Middle Eastern favorite

10 ml	2	teasp. salt
	2	cloves garlic, crushed
60 ml	¼	cup Sunlite Oil
15 ml	1	Tablesp. fresh lemon juice
5 ml	1	teasp. each: crushed oregano and thyme
5 ml	1	teasp. paprika
3 ml	½	teasp. pepper
2700 g	5	to 6-lb. leg of lamb

In a small bowl, mash salt and garlic to a paste. Stir in Sunlite Oil, lemon juice and seasonings. Place lamb on rack in a shallow roasting pan. Rub entire surface with herb mixture. Roast at 325°F 30 to 35 minutes per pound (about 2½ to 3 hrs.) or until meat thermometer registers 175° to 180°F; baste often. Allow to stand 5 to 10 minutes before carving. Makes 8 to 10 servings.

pan glazed fruit

Perfect compliment to an intimate dinner

	1	tart red apple
	2	firm, ripe bananas
		Sunlite Oil
85 ml	⅓	cup brown sugar
	4	slices canned pineapple, halved
30 ml	2	Tablesp. pineapple juice
5 ml	1	teasp. lemon juice
5 ml	1	teasp. cornstarch
1 ml	¼	teasp. cinnamon
	4	walnut halves, sliced

Wash and core apple; cut in ½-inch wedges. Peel and cut bananas in half lengthwise and again crosswise. Coat apple wedges with Sunlite Oil; sprinkle with *3 to 4 tablespoons* brown sugar. Cook in a heavy skillet over medium heat about 10 minutes; stir occasionally. When almost tender, add pieces of banana and pineapple slice halves. Sprinkle with *remaining* brown sugar. Cook a few minutes longer; turn fruit once or twice until glazed and heated through. Move fruit to one side of skillet. Combine pineapple juice, lemon juice, cornstarch and cinnamon. Stir into pan juices and cook quickly, stirring, until slightly thickened. Stir in walnuts; spoon over fruit. Makes 4 to 6 servings.

eggplant parma

Budget dish with Italian flair

	1 medium eggplant, cut in ½-inch cubes
60 ml	¼ cup minced onion
45 ml	3 Tablesp. Sunlite Oil
125 ml	½ cup fine dry bread crumbs
60 ml	¼ cup grated Parmesan cheese
30 ml	2 Tablesp. minced parsley
3 ml	½ teasp. oregano
3 ml	½ teasp. salt
425 g	1 (15-oz.) can tomato sauce
110 g	4 ozs. mozzarella cheese, sliced thinly

In a small skillet, sauté eggplant and onion in Sunlite Oil 3 to 5 minutes tossing to coat eggplant; set aside. In a small bowl, mix together bread crumbs, Parmesan, parsley, oregano and salt. Add to eggplant and toss gently to mix. In a lightly oiled 1½-quart baking dish, place *half* the eggplant, *half* the tomato sauce and *half* the mozzarella. Repeat layers using *remaining* ingredients. Bake at 400°F 30 to 35 minutes until tender. Makes 4 to 6 servings.

broccoli au gratin

All-time favorite cooked a bright new way

450 g	1 lb. fresh or frozen broccoli
60 ml	¼ cup Sunlite Oil
5 ml	1 teasp. salt
30 ml	2 Tablesp. flour
250 ml	1 cup milk
250 ml	1 cup shredded sharp Cheddar cheese
5 ml	1 teasp. prepared mustard
15 ml	1 Tablesp. imitation bacon bits

Wash broccoli; thaw if frozen. Cut flowerettes from stalks. Cut stalks in ¼-inch slices. Heat *2 tablespoons* Sunlite Oil in heavy skillet or electric fry pan at 350°F. Add broccoli *slices;* stir; cover and cook 5 minutes. Add flowerettes; stir; cover and cook 10 minutes longer until crisp-tender. Sprinkle with ½ *teaspoon* salt. Meanwhile, blend *2 tablespoons* Sunlite Oil with flour and ½ *teaspoon* salt in a saucepan. Add milk gradually, stirring. Cook over medium heat, stirring, until mixture comes to a boil and is slightly thickened and smooth. Stir in cheese and mustard until well blended and cheese is melted. Spoon over broccoli; sprinkle with bacon bits. Makes 4 servings.

glorious fish and poultry

Deliciously different, Lite alternatives to meat

Sensational dine-in masterpiece

450 g	1	lb. large raw shrimp, cleaned
	8	green beans, ends trimmed
	4	mushroom caps
	4	green onions, trimmed to 4-inch lengths
	2	zucchini, sliced ¼ inch thick
	1	large yam, peeled and thinly sliced
250 ml	1	cup ice water
250 ml	1	cup flour
	1	egg yolk
30 ml	2	Tablesp. Sunlite Oil
5 ml	1	teasp. sugar
3 ml	½	teasp. salt
3 ml	½	teasp. baking powder
		Sunlite Oil for frying
500 ml	2	cups hot cooked rice
250 ml	1	cup Oriental Dip (recipe below)

Wash shrimp; pat dry. Prepare vegetables; wash and pat dry. Refrigerate. In a blender or bowl, combine ice water with *next 6 ingredients;* whip until smooth; refrigerate. Fill wok, deep-fry pan or large, deep skillet ⅓ full with Sunlite Oil. Heat to 375°F and maintain temperature with deep-fry thermometer. Dip shrimp and vegetables, a few at a time, in batter, letting excess drain off, then into heated oil. Fry 2 to 3 minutes until light golden. Keep warm in low oven on paper-towel-covered cookie sheet until frying is completed. Arrange tempura on hot cooked rice; serve dip, warm, on the side. Makes 4 servings.

Oriental Dip: In a small saucepan, heat together ¾ cup water, ¼ cup soy sauce, 2 to 3 tablespoons honey, 1 tablespoon Sunlite Oil, ½ teaspoon ground ginger and ½ chicken bouillon cube. Makes 1 cup.

sautéed fillets almondine

Quickly cooked, uniquely sauced

675 g	1½ lbs. thin fish fillets such as sole, turbot, halibut, red snapper, etc.
30 ml	2 Tablesp. milk
45 ml	3 Tablesp. flour
15 ml	1 Tablesp. cornmeal
5 ml	1 teasp. salt
.5 ml	⅛ teasp. pepper
60 ml	¼ cup Sunlite Oil
45 ml	3 Tablesp. slivered almonds
30 ml	2 Tablesp. lemon juice
15 ml	1 Tablesp. minced parsley

Thaw fillets, if frozen; cut into serving-size pieces; pat dry. Brush with milk; coat on both sides with mixture of flour, cornmeal, salt and pepper. Heat large skillet a few minutes over medium heat. Add Sunlite Oil to skillet. Sauté fillets in hot oil about 3 minutes *on each side* until lightly browned. Remove to warm platter. In same skillet, brown almonds lightly. Add lemon juice; heat quickly and pour over fillets. Sprinkle with parsley. Makes 4 servings.

baked salmon strata

Spectacular budget stretcher

440 g	1 (15½-oz.) can salmon, drained
60 ml	¼ cup minced onion
	1 clove garlic, minced
30 ml	2 Tablesp. Sunlite Oil
	8 slices (½ inch thick) French bread
	Margarine
225 g	½ lb. Cheddar cheese, diced
375 ml	1½ cups milk
	4 eggs, slightly beaten
5 ml	1 teasp. seasoned salt
1 ml	¼ teasp. paprika

In a saucepan, sauté onion and garlic in Sunlite Oil. Add salmon; toss to mix; set aside. Spread bread slices on one side with margarine; cut into small cubes. In 1½-quart oiled casserole, place layers of *half* the bread, *half* the cheese and *half* the salmon mixture. Repeat layers with *remaining* bread, cheese and salmon. Combine the milk and *remaining* ingredients; pour over salmon-mixture layers. Let stand 15 minutes, pressing gently to immerse all ingredients. Bake at 350°F 1 hour until golden brown and slightly puffed. Serve at once. Makes 6 servings.

savory seafood chowder

Full-flavored and hearty entrée soup

85 ml	⅓	cup each: diced onion and celery
60 ml	¼	cup finely chopped green pepper
	1	clove garlic, minced
60 ml	¼	cup Sunlite Oil
450 g	1	(16-oz.) can cream-style corn
305 g	1	(10¾-oz.) can condensed cream of potato soup
125 ml	½	cup dry white wine or water
625 ml	2½	cups milk
10 ml	2	teasp. seasoned salt
5 ml	1	teasp. fines herbes
.5 ml	⅛	teasp. pepper
	1	small bay leaf
185 g	1	(6½-oz.) can minced clams, drained
110 g	4	ozs. cooked or canned small bay shrimp
60 ml	¼	cup imitation bacon bits

In a 2-quart kettle, sauté onion, celery, green pepper and garlic in Sunlite Oil until crisp-tender. Add corn, potato soup, wine and milk; mix well. Stir in remaining ingredients *except bacon bits.* Heat to simmer, stirring. Simmer, *do not boil,* 10 minutes; stir occasionally. Remove bay leaf. Top servings with bacon bits. Makes 6 (about 1 cup) servings.

superb tuna quiche

Serve hot for main dish, cold for appetizer

85 ml	⅓	cup each: chopped onion and green pepper
85 ml	⅓	cup sliced mushrooms
45 ml	3	Tablesp. Sunlite Oil
200 g	1	(7-oz.) can tuna packed in water, drained
15 ml	1	Tablesp. minced parsley
3 ml	½	teasp. tarragon
	3	eggs, slightly beaten
250 ml	1	cup milk
15 ml	1	Tablesp. sherry (optional)
5 ml	1	teasp. salt
125 ml	½	cup shredded Swiss cheese
23 cm	1	(9-inch) unbaked Sunlite single crust (p. 68).

In a small skillet, sauté onion, green pepper and mushrooms in Sunlite Oil until crisp-tender. Add tuna, parsley and tarragon; toss to mix; set aside. In a small bowl, combine eggs, milk, sherry and salt; mix well; set aside. Sprinkle cheese over bottom of pie shell. Arrange tuna mixture over cheese. Pour egg and milk mixture gradually over all. Bake at 425°F 10 minutes; *reduce temperature* to 325°F; bake 40 to 45 minutes longer until set. Let stand 5 minutes before cutting. Makes 4 to 6 servings or cut in 12 wedges for appetizers.

broiled and sauced fish

Seafood at its classic best

675 g	1½	lbs. thin fish fillets *or* (½ to 1-inch) thick fish steaks *or* (2- to 3-lb.) whole fish
45 ml	3	Tablesp. Sunlite Oil
30 ml	2	Tablesp. lemon juice
3 ml	½	teasp. salt
1 ml	¼	teasp. marjoram or thyme
.5 ml	⅛	teasp. pepper

Choose fish such as sole, halibut, turbot, red snapper, sea bass or flounder; thaw if frozen. Use a broil and serve platter, small foil broiler pan, or foil-lined broiler pan. Preheat oven at "broil" 5 to 10 minutes. In a small bowl, combine Sunlite Oil and *remaining* ingredients. Brush over fish of choice.

For Thin Fish Fillets: broil 2 inches from heat about 6 to 7 minutes; *do not turn.* Makes 4 to 6 servings.

For ½ to 1-Inch Fish Steaks: broil 2 inches from heat for 5 minutes; turn, baste fish; broil 5 to 10 minutes longer depending on thickness. Makes 4 to 6 servings.

For 2 to 3-lb. Whole Dressed Fish: broil 3 inches from heat if thin like flounder, 6 inches if thick like red snapper; about 6 minutes. Turn, baste; broil 8 to 10 minutes longer depending on thickness. Makes 6 servings.

Garnish as desired and serve with Tartar Sauce (p. 15) or one of the following sauces—

Cucumber Sauce: Combine ½ *cup Sunlite Mayonnaise (p. 15) with* ½ *cup* finely diced peeled cucumber, ¼ *teaspoon* onion salt and ¼ *teaspoon* celery seed. Makes ⅔ cup.

Spicy Lemon Sauce: Combine ⅓ *cup* Sunlite Mayonnaise (p. 15) with *2 tablespoons* lemon juice and 1 teaspoon <u>each:</u> prepared horseradish, prepared mustard and minced onion. Makes ⅓ cup.

Baked fish is equally delicious. Baste fish; arrange on lemon slices in baking dish. Bake at 425° to 450°F 20 to 30 minutes. Do not overcook.

stuffed fillets florentine

Delicious spinach stuffing makes this special

284 g	1	(10-oz.) pkg. frozen chopped spinach
250 ml	1	cup ricotta or cottage cheese
60 ml	¼	cup minced onion
	1	egg, slightly beaten
3 ml	½	teasp. salt
3 ml	½	teasp. oregano
560 g	6	(about 1¼-lbs.) fish fillets such as sole, perch, halibut, etc.
		Sunlite Oil
		Salt and pepper
	1½	slices day-old bread, crumbled
15 ml	1	Tablesp. minced parsley
125 ml	½	cup Curry Dressing (p. 15)

Cook spinach as package directs; drain thoroughly; press excess moisture with paper towel. Combine, in a bowl, with ricotta, onion, egg, salt and oregano; mix well; set aside. Brush fillets lightly with Sunlite Oil; sprinkle with salt and pepper. Spread stuffing evenly over each; roll up pinwheel fashion. Arrange in lightly oiled 1½-quart baking dish pinwheel-side up. Toss bread with parsley and ½ *teaspoon* Sunlite Oil; sprinkle over fillets. Bake at 400°F 25 to 30 minutes until easily flaked with a fork. Serve with Curry Dressing. Makes 4 to 6 servings.

tuna creole in rice ring

Family favorite all dressed up

	1	small green pepper, cut in ½-inch squares
125 ml	½	cup sliced celery
125 ml	½	cup coarsely chopped onion
	1	clove garlic, minced
45 ml	3	Tablesp. Sunlite Oil
410 g	1	(14½-oz.) can stewed tomatoes
5 ml	1	teasp. thyme
3 ml	½	teasp. salt
	1	small bay leaf
	1	dash Tabasco
200 g	1	(7-oz.) can tuna packed in water, drained
750 ml	3	cups hot cooked rice

In a medium skillet, sauté green pepper, celery, onion and garlic in Sunlite Oil until crisp-tender. Add stewed tomatoes and seasonings; simmer 10 minutes; stir occasionally. Stir in tuna in chunks; heat through. Remove bay leaf. Pack rice into lightly oiled 1-quart ring mold; turn out on serving platter. Spoon tuna creole into center. Makes 4 servings.

creamy chicken soup *(illustrated opposite)*

Half a chicken goes a long way

	½	frying chicken, cut up
2 l	2	quarts water
		Salt
	1	small onion, chopped
	3	ribs celery, sliced
60 ml	¼	cup Sunlite Oil
45 ml	3	Tablesp. flour
1 ml	¼	teasp. pepper
500 ml	2	cups uncooked thin egg noodles
125 ml	½	cup half-and-half

In a Dutch oven, cover chicken with water, add *2 teaspoons* salt and bring to boil. Reduce heat and simmer, covered, until tender, about 40 minutes. Remove chicken, reserving broth. Bone and shred chicken, discarding skin and bones. Meanwhile, in a skillet, sauté onion and celery in Sunlite Oil until transparent. Stir in flour, *1 teaspoon* salt and pepper and cook, stirring, until golden brown. Add to reserved broth; bring to boil and stir in noodles. Simmer about 10 minutes. Add chicken and half-and-half; heat through. Makes 6 servings.

chicken salad casserole

Serve with crescent rolls and fruit

	3	ribs celery, sliced
	1	small onion, chopped
30 ml	2	Tablesp. Sunlite Oil
500 ml	2	cups cubed, cooked chicken
125 ml	½	cup slivered almonds, coarsely chopped
56 g	1	(2-oz.) can sliced ripe olives
375 ml	1½	cups shredded Cheddar cheese
250 ml	1	cup Sunlite Mayonnaise (p. 15)
5 ml	1	teasp. seasoned salt
5 ml	1	teasp. dill weed
1 ml	¼	teasp. pepper

In a 10-inch skillet, sauté celery and onion in Sunlite Oil until crisp-tender. Add remaining ingredients *except ½ cup* cheese; mix well. Pour into a small casserole; top with *remaining* cheese. Bake at 350°F 25 minutes or until bubbly. Makes 6 servings.

herbed game hens

Tender, flavorful and juicy

15 ml	1	Tablesp. seasoned salt
5 ml	1	teasp. thyme
3 ml	½	teasp. <u>each:</u> rosemary and tarragon
1 ml	¼	teasp. pepper
60 ml	¼	cup Sunlite Oil
	4	Cornish Game Hens

Combine salt, herbs and oil in a small bowl. Thaw game hens if frozen; rub hens inside and out with equal portions of herb mixture; truss. Roast at 400°F 50 minutes or until inside juices run clear. Turn and baste about every 15 minutes, ending with breast-side up. Makes 4 servings.

Turn bird breast-side up; fill cavity loosely with stuffing.

Insert 2 to 3-inch skewers across cavity opening 1-inch apart.

Double a heavy string 4 times the length of the opening. Loop around top skewer and lace toward tail vent. Cross the string ends and loop underneath tail, then over and around opposite drumstick. Draw drumsticks and tail tightly together; tie a knot to secure.

44

roast chicken with stuffing

Great with your favorite bread stuffing

1350 g	2½	to 3-lb. whole frying chicken
	1	small onion, chopped
125 ml	½	cup snipped parsley
	1	clove garlic, crushed
		Sunlite Oil
180 g	1	(6¼-oz.) pkg. quick-cooking long grain and wild rice
		Salt and pepper

Remove giblets from chicken; place giblets in a saucepan with enough water to cover and simmer until tender, about 45 minutes. Remove and chop finely; reserve broth. In a large saucepan, sauté giblets, onion, parsley and garlic in *3 tablespoons* Sunlite Oil. Add rice and seasoning packet, and reserved broth *plus* enough water to make 2 cups; cook according to package directions for rice. Meanwhile, season chicken with salt and pepper. Stuff with rice mixture, truss* and rub with Sunlite Oil, salt and pepper. Roast on rack in a shallow baking pan at 425°F 15 minutes; *reduce temperature* to 350°F and roast 1 hour longer, basting frequently. (Thigh should measure 180°F on meat thermometer.) Makes 4 servings.

*See page 44 on how to truss

chicken and broccoli casserole

Just a hint of curry

	4	chicken breast halves, skinned and boned
125 ml	½	cup flour
60 ml	¼	cup Sunlite Oil
500 ml	2	cups broccoli spears, cooked and drained
284 g	1	(10-oz.) can cream of chicken soup
250 ml	1	cup Sunlite Mayonnaise (p. 15)
375 ml	1½	cups shredded Cheddar cheese
60 ml	¼	cup milk
1 ml	¼	teasp. curry powder
500 ml	2	cups croutons

Coat chicken pieces with flour in plastic bag. Heat Sunlite Oil in a 10-inch skillet over medium heat. Add chicken pieces and sauté until slightly brown and tender; drain on paper towels. Place broccoli in a large glass baking dish; top with chicken. Combine *remaining* ingredients *except* croutons; pour over chicken. Top with croutons. Bake at 350°F 25 to 30 minutes or until "bubbly." Makes 4 servings.

southern fried chicken

A tradition in many families

85 ml	⅓	cup flour
15 ml	1	Tablesp. seasoned salt
1 ml	¼	teasp. pepper
1350 g	2½	to 3-lb. frying chicken, cut up
		Sunlite Oil

Combine flour, salt and pepper in plastic bag. Drop in chicken, a few pieces at a time; shake to coat. Heat Sunlite Oil ½ inch deep in a 12-inch or electric skillet to 350°F. Fry chicken, skin-side down, 15 to 20 minutes. Turn; fry 15 to 20 minutes longer until tender. Makes 4 servings.

fried crumbed chicken

For an extra crispy crust

1350 g	2½	to 3-lb. frying chicken, cut up
		Salt and pepper
125 ml	½	cup flour
	1	egg, beaten with ¼ *cup* water
500 ml	2	cups fine dry bread crumbs
		Sunlite Oil

Season chicken with salt and pepper. Dredge pieces in flour, dip in egg mixture, then roll in bread crumbs until well coated. Heat Sunlite Oil ½ inch deep in a 12-inch or electric skillet to 350°F. Fry chicken 15 to 20 minutes *on each side* until tender. Makes 4 servings.

batter fried chicken

Beer in the batter for lightness

180 ml	¾	cup beer
125 ml	½	cup flour
10 ml	1½	teasp. seasoned salt
		Sunlite Oil
1350 g	2½	to 3-lb. frying chicken, cut up

In a medium bowl, combine beer, flour and salt; beat until smooth. Fill a Dutch oven or heavy kettle ⅓ full with Sunlite Oil. Heat to 350°F and maintain temperature with deep-fry thermometer. Lightly coat chicken pieces with flour, then dip in batter. Fry, a few pieces at a time, in hot oil until golden brown, about 10 minutes. Makes 4 servings.

chicken paprikash

A Hungarian specialty

	1	large onion, chopped
	½	green pepper, chopped
30 ml	2	Tablesp. Sunlite Oil
15 ml	1	Tablesp. paprika
5 ml	1	teasp. salt
1 ml	¼	teasp. pepper
1350 g	2½	to 3-lb. frying chicken, cut up
425 g	1	(15-oz.) can tomato sauce with tomato bits
250 ml	1	cup water
225 g	8	ozs. bow tie noodles, cooked and drained
225 g	8	ozs. sour cream

In a Dutch oven, sauté onion and green pepper in Sunlite Oil over medium heat until tender. Remove pan from heat; add paprika, salt and pepper. Return pan to heat and add chicken. Cook 10 to 15 minutes, stirring frequently. Add tomato sauce and water; simmer, *covered,* 25 to 30 minutes longer; stir occasionally. Remove chicken from pan and arrange on serving platter over noodles. Skim excess fat from sauce. Mix ½ *cup* sour cream and ½ *cup* sauce in a small bowl; stir and return back into sauce gradually. Ladle over chicken and noodles; dollop with *remaining* sour cream. Makes 4 to 6 servings.

turkey pie

Economical and good tasting

	1	recipe Sunlite double-crust Pastry (p. 68)
250 ml	1	cup sliced mushrooms
	1	small onion, chopped
30 ml	2	Tablesp. Sunlite Oil
675 ml	2½	cups cooked, shredded turkey
284 g	1	(10-oz.) pkg. frozen peas and carrots, cooked and drained
284 g	1	(10-oz.) can cream of chicken soup
125 ml	½	cup sour cream
60 ml	¼	cup water
5 ml	1	teasp. seasoned salt
1 ml	¼	teasp. pepper

Roll out all of dough between wax paper into 13 × 9-inch rectangle; set aside. In a 10-inch skillet, sauté mushrooms and onion in Sunlite Oil until onion is transparent. Add *remaining* ingredients and simmer 5 minutes. Pour mixture into 7 × 11-inch glass baking dish. Peel off top paper from pastry; place paper-side up over baking dish. Peel off paper. Trim overhanging edge 1 inch from edge of dish; flute edges. Decorate top with leftover dough, if desired. Bake at 425°F 25 to 30 minutes. Makes 6 to 8 servings.

beignets *(illustrated opposite)*

"French Market" doughnuts

	1 pkg. dry yeast
180 ml	¾ cup warm water
60 ml	¼ cup sugar
3 ml	½ teasp. salt
	1 egg
125 ml	½ cup evaporated milk
875 ml	3½ cups sifted all-purpose flour
	Sunlite Oil
	Powdered sugar

In a large bowl, dissolve yeast in water; add sugar, salt, egg and milk. Gradually stir in *2 cups* flour. Beat until smooth; work in *remaining* flour ¼ *cup* at a time, kneading to form a smooth, firm dough. Cover with damp towel and refrigerate overnight. Roll out dough ¼-inch thick on a lightly floured board; cut into 2½ × 3½-inch rectangles. Fill a heavy kettle or Dutch oven ⅓ full with oil. Heat to 375°F and maintain temperature with deep-fry thermometer. Gently add a few pieces of dough, one at a time. Fry 1 to 2 minutes until golden brown. Drain on paper towels. To serve, sprinkle with powdered sugar. Makes about 22 beignets.

chicken and asparagus pie

Left over chicken made special

284 g	20 fresh *or* 1 (10-oz.) pkg. frozen asparagus spears, cooked
23 cm	1 (9-inch) unbaked Sunlite single crust (p. 68)
375 ml	1½ cups chopped, cooked chicken
	4 slices bacon, cooked and crumbled
180 ml	¾ cup shredded Swiss cheese
	4 eggs
15 ml	1 Tablesp. flour
3 ml	½ teasp. seasoned salt
250 ml	1 cup light cream
30 ml	2 Tablesp. grated Parmesan cheese
	Paprika

Arrange asparagus spears spoke-fashion in bottom of pie shell. Top with chicken. Sprinkle with bacon and Swiss cheese. In a small bowl, beat eggs with flour, salt and cream until well mixed; pour over asparagus and cheese mixture. Sprinkle with Parmesan cheese and paprika. Bake at 375°F 45 to 50 minutes or until set in center. Let stand 10 minutes before cutting. Makes 8 servings.

veal piccata

Classic dish traditionally prepared

900 g	2	lbs. sliced veal or boneless chicken breasts
		Seasoned salt and fresh ground pepper
		Flour
125 ml	½	cup Sunlite Oil
		Juice of 2 lemons
30 ml	2	Tablesp. chopped fresh parsley
30 ml	2	Tablesp. margarine

Place veal slices between sheets of wax paper and pound very thin with flat side of a knife or meat mallet. Sprinkle with seasoned salt and pepper; cut in thin strips and dust with flour. Heat ¼ cup Sunlite Oil in a large skillet over high heat. Sauté *half* the veal strips quickly; remove; set aside, and sauté *remaining* veal strips. Remove. Add lemon juice and parsley to skillet; stir to deglaze pan. Remove from heat; swirl in *remaining* Sunlite Oil and the margarine. Return sautéed veal to skillet and toss gently to coat. Makes 6 to 8 servings.

halibut brochettes

Serve with fruit salad and simple dessert

675 g	1½	lbs. halibut or other firm, white fish steaks, 1-inch thick
	8	large mushroom caps
	1	medium green pepper, cut in 8 squares
	16	chunks fresh or canned pineapple
	4	(7-inch) skewers
85 ml	⅓	cup soy sauce
45 ml	3	Tablesp. Sunlite Oil
30 ml	2	Tablesp. honey
30 ml	2	Tablesp. water
15 ml	1	Tablesp. sherry
5 ml	1	teasp. ground ginger
624 g	2	(11-oz.) pkgs. frozen rice pilaf with peas and onions

Cut halibut into 12 portions. Alternate mushroom caps, halibut pieces, green pepper squares and pineapple chunks on skewers starting and ending with mushrooms on each. In a shallow baking dish combine soy sauce, Sunlite Oil, honey, water, sherry and ginger; mix thoroughly. Place brochettes in marinade, turning to coat on all sides. Refrigerate 1 hour; turn brochettes occasionally. Drain marinade; reserve. Bake at 400°F 20 to 25 minutes. Turn once or twice and baste with reserved marinade. Meanwhile, prepare rice pilaf as package directs. Arrange brochettes on pilaf to serve. Makes 4 servings.

walnut chicken

Serve over hot cooked rice

		Sunlite Oil
180 ml	¾	cup coarsely chopped walnuts
	3	chicken breast halves, skinned, boned and cut into 2-inch-long strips
	1	small onion, thinly sliced and separated into rings
	2	cloves garlic, crushed
	3	ribs celery, sliced on diagonal
	3	ribs bok choy, sliced on diagonal (optional)
110 g	¼	lb. bean sprouts
	2	chicken bouillon cubes
250 ml	1	cup hot water
30 ml	2	Tablesp. cornstarch
125 ml	½	cup cold water
30 ml	2	Tablesp. soy sauce

In a wok or 12-inch skillet, heat *1 tablespoon* Sunlite Oil over high heat. Add walnuts; stir and fry about 30 seconds. Remove from pan; set aside. Heat 1 *more tablespoon* oil in wok; add <u>half each:</u> chicken, onion and garlic; stir and fry until chicken is lightly browned. Remove from pan. Add *1 more tablespoon* oil and *repeat* with *remaining* chicken, onion and garlic. Remove from pan. Heat *2 more tablespoons* oil. Add vegetables; stir and fry until crisp-tender. Push vegetables up on sides of wok; add bouillon cubes mixed with *hot* water and cornstarch mixed with *cold* water and soy sauce. Cook and stir until thick and clear. Return chicken and walnuts to pan. Cook 1 minute longer. Makes 4 servings.

tabooley

Eastern salad with nutritious bulgur

125 ml	½	cup finely crushed bulgur wheat
		Water
	2	medium tomatoes, finely chopped
250 ml	1	cup finely chopped fresh parsley
85 ml	⅓	cup sliced radishes
125 ml	½	cup <u>each:</u> chopped onion and green pepper
8 ml	1½	teasp. salt
85 ml	⅓	cup fresh lemon juice
85 ml	⅓	cup Sunlite Oil
30 ml	2	Tablesp. finely chopped mint leaves

Place bulgur in a small bowl, add water to cover; set aside at least 30 to 40 minutes. Drain thoroughly. Combine in bowl with *remaining* ingredients; chill. Makes 6 to 8 servings.

puffy omelet *(illustrated opposite)*

Light, sweet dessert omelet

	4 eggs, separated
1 ml	¼ teasp. cream of tartar
60 ml	¼ cup cold water
30 ml	2 Tablesp. sugar
1 ml	¼ teasp. salt
30 ml	2 Tablesp. Sunlite Oil
125 ml	½ cup orange marmalade
	Powdered sugar

In a large bowl, beat egg *whites* until foamy; add cream of tartar and continue to beat until stiff peaks form. In a small bowl, beat egg *yolks* with water, sugar and salt, until light and fluffy; gradually fold yolk mixture into beaten egg whites. Heat Sunlite Oil in a 10-inch oven-proof skillet. Add egg mixture to skillet and cook about 3 minutes over medium heat until puffy and golden on underside. Place in oven preheated to 350°F; bake 10 minutes until golden and top springs back when touched with finger. Loosen edges with spatula. Make a slit partway across center of omelet; spoon in marmalade. Tip skillet and fold omelet in half; place on warm platter. Dust with powdered sugar. Makes 2 servings.

cinnamon nut coffee cake

Sour cream dresses up this brunch cake

250 ml	1 cup chopped walnuts
500 ml	2 cups brown sugar, packed
5 ml	1 teasp. cinnamon
3 ml	½ teasp. nutmeg
1 ml	¼ teasp. ground cloves
	Sifted all-purpose flour
	Sunlite Oil
	2 eggs
5 ml	1 teasp. <u>each</u>: baking powder and baking soda
3 ml	½ teasp. salt
225 g	1 (8-oz.) carton sour cream
125 ml	½ cup raisins

In a bowl, toss together walnuts, *1 cup* brown sugar, cinnamon, nutmeg, cloves and *1 tablespoon each* flour and Sunlite Oil; set aside. In a large bowl combine ½ *cup* Sunlite Oil, *1 cup* brown sugar and eggs. Beat 2 minutes on medium speed. Add *2 cups* flour and *remaining* ingredients *except* raisins; beat 2 minutes longer. Spread *half* the batter in an 8-inch-square greased pan; sprinkle with *half* the nut mixture. Top with raisins. Add *remaining* batter in a layer; sprinkle on *remaining* nut mixture. Bake at 350°F 40 to 45 minutes until toothpick inserted in center comes out clean. Makes 10 to 12 servings.

Parchment paper instead of foil for "purists"

	6 chicken breast halves, boned
	Salt and pepper
	Flour
60 ml	¼ cup Sunlite Oil
	Aluminum foil
	12 slices ham
	6 large mushroom caps
375 ml	1½ cups Marinara Sauce (p.55)
60 ml	¼ cup sweet Marsala wine or sherry

Sprinkle chicken with salt and pepper; dust lightly with flour. In a large skillet, sauté chicken quickly about 2 minutes on each side in Sunlite Oil. Cut foil in 6 large heart-shaped pieces. Place a slice of ham on *one half* of each foil heart. Top each with chicken breast and mushroom cap. Meanwhile, heat Marinara Sauce until "bubbly"; remove from heat; stir in wine. Spoon a generous portion of sauce mixture over each; top with *remaining* slices of ham. Fold the other half of the foil hearts over and double-fold edges to seal. Bake on cookie sheet at 450°F about 5 minutes. Makes 6 servings.

  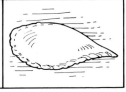

Place ham, chicken, mushroom and sauce *on half* of each foil heart.

Fold the *other half* of the foil heart over.

Double-fold edges to seal.

marinara sauce

Richly flavored, quickly simmered

125 ml	½	cup chopped onion
125 ml	½	cup chopped celery
	1	large clove garlic, minced
60 ml	¼	cup Sunlite Oil
820 g	2	(14½-oz.) cans stewed tomatoes
60 ml	¼	cup red wine (optional)
5 ml	1	teasp. salt
5 ml	1	teasp. basil
3 ml	½	teasp. oregano
1 ml	¼	teasp. pepper
	1	small bay leaf

In a 1½-quart saucepan, sauté onion, celery and garlic in Sunlite Oil until onion is transparent. Add tomatoes, crushing large pieces with a fork. Add *remaining* ingredients and simmer, covered, 15 minutes; stir occasionally. Remove bay leaf. Makes 1 quart sauce.

Note: Excellent cooking sauce ingredient, or serve over hot cooked pasta. Store in covered, non-metal container in refrigerator up to 2 weeks.

huevos rancheros

Perfect for a Mexican brunch

45 ml	3	Tablesp. Sunlite Oil
	4	corn tortillas
125 ml	½	cup chopped onion
	2	cloves garlic, minced
425 g	1	(15-oz.) can tomato sauce
110 g	1	(4-oz.) can diced green chilies
3 ml	½	teasp. seasoned salt
3 ml	½	teasp. cumin
	4	eggs
180 ml	¾	cup shredded Cheddar cheese
		Guacamole (p.15) (optional)

Heat Sunlite Oil in a medium skillet. Fry tortillas one at a time (about 20 seconds) just until heated, but not crisp; turn once. Drain on paper towels; set aside. In the same skillet, sauté onion and garlic until onion is transparent. Add tomato sauce, green chilies, salt and cumin; heat until "bubbly." *Reduce heat* and simmer 15 minutes longer. Meanwhile, in a small skillet, fry eggs one at a time, sunny-side up, in a little Sunlite Oil. Place on tortillas on individual oven-proof serving plates. Top with hot sauce. Sprinkle with cheese. Place under broiler just until cheese melts. Top with Guacamole. Makes 4 servings.

jambalaya *(illustrated opposite)*

A favorite from New Orleans

500 ml	2	cups chopped onion
	1	small green pepper, chopped
	1	clove garlic, minced
30 ml	2	Tablesp. minced parsley
250 ml	1	cup chopped ham
	4	Polish sausages, sliced
30 ml	2	Tablesp. Sunlite Oil
3 ml	½	teasp. salt
.5 ml	⅛	teasp. cayenne
	1	bay leaf
1 ml	¼	teasp. each: thyme and ground cloves
375 ml	1½	cups long grain rice
750 ml	3	cups beef broth
500 ml	1	pint fresh shucked oysters, drained
125 ml	¼	to ½ cup water, if necessary
225 g	8	ozs. uncooked shrimp, cleaned

In a large heavy Dutch oven or kettle, sauté the vegetables, parsley, ham and sausage in Sunlite Oil 15 minutes over low heat, stirring constantly. Add seasonings; mix thoroughly. Add rice; cook and stir over *medium* heat until rice is lightly browned. Add broth and oysters; mix gently. Bring to a boil; simmer, *uncovered,* 5 minutes. *Reduce heat,* cook, *covered* 20 minutes longer; stir often and add water, if needed. *Remove cover;* add shrimp; cook 10 minutes longer. Makes 6 to 8 servings.

florentine soufflé

Lovely, light and delicious

125 ml	½	cup Sunlite Oil
125 ml	½	cup sifted flour
8 ml	1½	teasp. seasoned salt
3 ml	½	teasp. each: cayenne and paprika
500 ml	2	cups milk
225 g	½	lb. Cheddar cheese, diced
	8	eggs, separated
375 ml	1½	cups fresh spinach, chopped, cooked and pressed dry

In a large saucepan, combine first 5 ingredients; mix well. Stir in milk gradually. Simmer over low heat, stirring constantly, until sauce is very thick. Add cheese; stir and cook over low heat until cheese melts. Remove from heat; stir in egg *yolks,* briskly with wire whip. Meanwhile, beat egg *whites* until stiff and dry. Gently fold in cheese sauce and spinach. Pour into a 2½-quart soufflé dish; bake 10 minutes in oven *preheated* to 425°F. *Reduce heat* to 400°F, bake 25 minutes longer. Serve at once. Makes 8 servings.

beef wellington

Sauced in the classic manner from Southern France

900 g	1	(2-lb.) beef tenderloin, trimmed
15 ml	1	Tablesp. Sunlite Oil
5 ml	1	teasp. salt
1 ml	¼	teasp. freshly ground pepper
	1	recipe Sunlite single-crust Pastry (p. 68)
	1	egg white, beaten with 1 *teasp.* water
77 g	1	(2¾-oz.) can liver paté
		Périgueux Sauce (recipe below)

Rub beef with Sunlite Oil, salt and pepper. Roast on rack in a shallow pan at 450°F for 20 minutes. Prepare pastry; roll out into rectangle large enough to wrap around beef, allowing ½-inch overlap; brush with egg-white mixture. Spread top of partially cooked beef with liver paté. Place paté-side down in center of pastry; wrap around beef, pressing edges together firmly to seal. Place *seam-side down* on baking sheet. Bake at 425°F 10 minutes. *Reduce* temperature to 375°F. Bake 20 to 30 minutes longer (depending on doneness desired) until crust is golden. Let stand 15 minutes before carving. Serve, sliced, with Périgueux Sauce. Makes 6 servings.

Périgueux Sauce: In a skillet, sauté *1 tablespoon* minced shallots and ½ *cup* sliced mushrooms in 2 tablespoons Sunlite Oil. Stir in *2 tablespoons* flour. Add *1 cup* water and *2 tablespoons* Madeira wine to any pan drippings from Wellington. Stir into skillet mixture. Cook until slightly thickened. Makes about *1½ cups* sauce.

---

monte cristos

Serve warm with jam or marmalade

12	slices white bread
8	slices mozzarella or American cheese
4	slices ham
4	slices turkey
	Sunlite Oil
6	eggs, well beaten
	Powdered sugar

Make 4 double-decker sandwiches using 3 slices of bread layered with ham and cheese, and turkey and cheese. Heat Sunlite Oil, ½ inch deep, in a large skillet to 375°F. Dip each sandwich into egg, coating both sides thoroughly. Fry until golden brown, turning once. Drain on paper towels. Sprinkle lightly with powdered sugar. Makes 4 sandwiches.

celebration crêpes

Leftovers in disguise

296 g	2	(10½-oz.) cans cream of chicken soup
170 ml	⅔	cup milk
125 ml	½	cup sherry
30 ml	2	Tablesp. chopped parsley
125 ml	½	cup chopped onion
60 ml	¼	cup Sunlite Oil
1000 ml	4	cups chopped, cooked turkey or chicken
750 ml	3	cups chopped tart, red-skinned apples
3 ml	½	teasp. salt
	16	warm Whole Wheat Crêpes (recipe below)

Combine soup, milk, sherry and parsley in saucepan. Simmer 5 minutes, stirring frequently. Meanwhile, in a large skillet, sauté onion in Sunlite Oil until transparent. Stir in turkey, apple and salt. Cook 5 minutes, stirring occasionally. Add *1 cup* sauce to turkey mixture; blend well. Place about ¼ *cup* filling on each crêpe; roll up. Serve seam-side down with *remaining* sauce spooned over. Makes 8 servings.

Whole Wheat Crêpes. In a bowl, combine *2 well-beaten* eggs and salt. Gradually add ½ *cup each:* all-purpose and whole wheat flour alternately with *1¼ cups* milk; beat until smooth. Stir in *2 tablespoons* Sunlite Oil. Refrigerate batter at least 1 hour. Cook *2 to 3 tablespoons* batter in a lightly-oiled 6- to 7-inch crêpe pan or heavy skillet over medium high heat, until browned; turn and brown other side. Makes about 16 crêpes.

blueberry muffins

Serve hot for Sunday brunch

500 ml	2	cups sifted cake flour
4 ml	¾	teasp. salt
180 ml	¾	cup sugar
10 ml	2	teasp. baking powder
	2	eggs, beaten
125 ml	½	cup Sunlite Oil
180 ml	¾	cup milk
450 g	1	(16-oz.) can blueberries, rinsed, drained and lightly floured

In a bowl, combine all ingredients *except* blueberries; beat 20 to 30 seconds, leaving some lumps. Gently fold in blueberries. Bake in a paper-lined muffin tin 20 to 25 minutes at 400°F. Makes about 2 dozen muffins.

chicken kiev

Make ahead of time for easy company dish

125 ml	½ cup margarine, softened
	1 clove garlic, finely minced
10 ml	2 teasp. each: minced chives and parsley
3 ml	½ teasp. salt
	6 large chicken breast halves, skinned and boned
60 ml	¼ cup flour
	1 egg, slightly beaten
15 ml	1 Tablesp. water
125 ml	½ cup fine, dry bread crumbs
	Sunlite Oil

In a small bowl, combine margarine, garlic, chives, parsley and salt; mix thoroughly. Form into ¾-inch-thick roll on wax paper; wrap; chill until very firm. With a rolling pin, gently flatten chicken to ¼-inch thickness. Cut chilled roll of margarine mixture in 6 portions. Place one in center of each chicken breast half; roll up tightly, tucking in ends; secure with toothpicks. Dip each in flour, then in egg mixed with water, then in bread crumbs, until well coated. *Chill thoroughly.* In a large skillet, heat Sunlite Oil, ¾ to 1 inch deep, to 350°F. Add chicken rolls; fry, turning occasionally, about 10 to 15 minutes, until golden brown on all sides. Drain on paper towel. Remove toothpicks to serve. Makes 6 servings.

oriental crab toss

On the table in 20 minutes

170 g	1 (6-oz.) pkg. frozen crab meat, thawed
170 g	1 (6-oz.) pkg. frozen Chinese pea pods and water chestnuts, partially thawed
250 ml	1 cup fresh or canned bean sprouts
	1 small onion, sliced, separated into rings
45 ml	3 Tablesp. Sunlite Oil
125 ml	½ cup water
	1 chicken bouillon cube
10 ml	2 teasp. each: cornstarch and soy sauce
1 ml	¼ teasp. ground ginger
500 ml	2 cups hot cooked rice

Drain and reserve liquid from crab meat. In a wok or 10-inch skillet, sauté crab meat and next three ingredients in Sunlite Oil, until onion is transparent. Add water and bouillon cube; simmer, uncovered, until pea pods are just crisp-tender (about 5 minutes); stir occasionally. Blend together cornstarch, crab-meat liquid, soy sauce and ginger; stir into crab mixture. Simmer a minute or two longer until slightly thickened. Serve immediately on hot cooked rice. Makes 4 servings.

caribbean chicken and spaghetti

Chicken and pasta with Island flavor

1350 g	2½ to 3 lbs. frying chicken pieces	
45 ml	3 Tablesp. Sunlite Oil	
	Salt and pepper	
	1 medium onion, thinly sliced	
	1 clove garlic, minced	
30 ml	2 Tablesp. chopped cilantro or parsley	
170 g	1 (6-oz.) can tomato paste	
500 ml	2 cups water	
60 ml	¼ cup dark rum or brandy	
225 g	8 ozs. spaghetti, cooked and drained	

In a large skillet, brown chicken on all sides in Sunlite Oil. Remove chicken; sprinkle with salt and pepper; set aside. In same skillet, sauté onion, garlic and cilantro in drippings until onion is soft. Drain fat. Return chicken to skillet. In a small bowl, combine tomato paste, water and rum; mix well. Pour over chicken. Cover; simmer 25 to 30 minutes until chicken is tender. Arrange spaghetti on a large serving platter; place chicken pieces in center; pour sauce over all. Makes 4 to 6 servings.

vegetable paella

An elaborate Spanish dish

60 ml	¼ cup Sunlite Oil	
250 ml	1 cup chopped onion	
	2 ripe tomatoes, chopped	
	1 each: red and green pepper, chopped	
375 ml	1½ cups long grain rice	
5 ml	1 teasp. salt	
3 ml	½ teasp. freshly ground pepper	
3 ml	½ teasp. crushed saffron	
	Dash of Tabasco	
750 ml	3 cups chicken stock or broth	
15 ml	1 Tablesp. tomato paste	
	12 asparagus spears, cut in 1-inch pieces	
	2 small zucchini, cut in 1-inch pieces	
340 g	¾ lb. broccoli, pared and cut in 1-inch pieces	
284 g	1 (10-oz.) pkg. frozen peas	

Heat Sunlite Oil in a 12-inch paella pan or heavy oven-proof skillet over medium heat; add onion, tomatoes, green and red peppers; sauté until soft. Stir in rice, salt, pepper, saffron, Tabasco, broth and tomato paste; mix thoroughly. Heat to boiling; remove from heat. Cover; bake in oven at 350°F 15 minutes. Stir in vegetables; cover; bake 10 to 15 minutes longer, until liquid is absorbed and rice is tender but not soft. Let stand, *uncovered,* 5 to 10 minutes. Serve directly from pan. Makes 6 to 8 servings.

delicious breads
and desserts

Quick and easy—Lite and tasty

chocolate crêpe gâteau *(Illustrated opposite)*

Gâteau means *cake* in French

750 ml	3	cups whipping cream, chilled
		Powdered sugar
15 ml	1	Tablesp. <u>each</u>: cocoa and crème de cacao liqueur
8 ml	1½	teasp. vanilla
20 ml	4	teasp. crème de menthe liqueur
	4	drops green food coloring
	16	Chocolate Crêpes (recipe below)
		Ground walnuts

Divide cream equally into 2 small mixing bowls. To one bowl, add ¼ *cup* powdered sugar, cocoa, crème de cacao and vanilla; beat until very stiff. To other bowl, add *1 tablespoon* powdered sugar, crème de menthe and food coloring; beat until very stiff. Center a crêpe on a small flat serving platter. Spread with a thin layer of *chocolate* filling. Press a crêpe on top and spread with a thin layer *crème de menthe* filling. Continue with alternating layers of crêpes and fillings, ending with a crêpe; trim the edges. Spread the *remaining chocolate* filling on the *sides* and the *remaining mint filling* on the *top*. Press ground nuts into sides and sprinkle lightly on top; chill. Cut into wedges for serving. Makes 8 servings.

chocolate crêpes

Serve chocolate sauce over ice-cream-filled crêpes

170 ml	⅔	cup milk
170 ml	⅔	cup water
	2	whole eggs
	2	egg yolks
250 ml	1	cup sifted flour
60 ml	¼	cup sugar
15 ml	1	Tablesp. sifted cocoa
5 ml	⅛	teasp. salt
15 ml	1	Tablesp. Sunlite Oil

Combine all ingredients in blender container; blend. Heat an 8-inch crêpe pan over medium heat; brush lightly with Sunlite Oil. Pour in *scant 3 tablespoons* batter, tilting pan to thinly coat bottom. Return to heat. When crêpe is lightly browned, turn and brown other side. Makes 16 crêpes.

banana nut waffles

Honey of a brunch entrée

430 ml	1¾	cups sifted all-purpose flour
5 ml	1	teasp. baking powder
5 ml	1	teasp. baking soda
500 ml	2	cups buttermilk
125 ml	½	cup Sunlite Oil
	2	eggs
	1	ripe banana
30 ml	2	Tablesp. brown sugar, firmly packed
250 ml	1	cup coarsely chopped pecans
		Honey of a Syrup (recipe below)

Heat waffle iron as manufacturer directs. In a blender jar, combine all ingredients *except* pecans and Honey of a Syrup; blend 1 minute; stir and blend 1 minute longer. With spatula, stir in nuts. When waffle iron is hot, pour batter in center until it spreads to about 1 inch from edges. Cover and bake according to manufacturer's directions. Loosen edge with fork. Serve at once with Honey of a Syrup. Makes 6 to 8 waffles.

Honey of a Syrup: Heat together *1 cup* honey, *½ cup* maple syrup and *1 teaspoon* cinnamon. Makes 1½ cups.

---

cowboy cookies

Favorite with "cowboys" of any age

250 ml	1	cup brown sugar, packed
125 ml	½	cup Sunlite Oil
	2	eggs
3 ml	½	teasp. <u>each</u>: cinnamon and nutmeg
250 ml	1	cup sifted all-purpose flour
125 ml	½	cup whole wheat flour
125 ml	½	cup quick-cooking oatmeal
3 ml	½	teasp. baking soda
3 ml	½	teasp. salt
250 ml	1	cup chopped dates
250 ml	1	cup raisins

In a large bowl, combine brown sugar, Sunlite Oil, eggs, cinnamon and nutmeg; blend thoroughly. Stir in all *remaining* ingredients until well mixed. Drop by rounded teaspoonfuls about 2 inches apart on ungreased cookie sheet. Bake at 375°F 8 to 10 minutes. Remove from cookie sheet immediately; cool on rack. Makes about 4 dozen cookies.

golden pound cake

Save egg whites for meringue shells

500 ml	2	cups sugar
250 ml	1	cup Sunlite Oil
875 ml	3½	cups sifted cake flour
10 ml	2	teasp. baking powder
3 ml	½	teasp. salt
250 ml	1	cup milk
	6	egg yolks
10 ml	2	teasp. vanilla

In a large mixing bowl, beat sugar and Sunlite Oil on *high* speed until light and fluffy. Add flour mixed with baking powder and salt, and remaining ingredients. Beat on *low* speed until well mixed, scraping bowl constantly with rubber spatula. Beat on *high* speed 4 minutes, scraping bowl occasionally. Pour into greased and floured 10-inch Bundt pan. Bake 1 hour at 350°F until toothpick inserted in center comes out clean. Cool cake in pan on a rack 10 minutes. Turn out on cake plate; cool completely. Makes 1 (10-inch) pound cake.

tipsy fudge brownies

Skip the "tipsy" for a traditional brownie

	3	eggs
250 ml	1	cup white sugar
250 ml	1	cup brown sugar, packed
84 g	3	ozs. unsweetened chocolate, melted and cooled
170 ml	⅔	cup Sunlite Oil
60 ml	¼	cup almond-flavored liqueur *or* water
375 ml	1½	cups sifted all-purpose flour
3 ml	½	teasp. baking powder
3 ml	½	teasp. salt
180 ml	¾	cup chopped walnuts

Combine eggs and sugars in a bowl; beat until light and well blended. Stir in melted chocolate, Sunlite Oil and liqueur. Add flour sifted with baking powder and salt; mix well. Stir in chopped nuts. Spread in a greased and floured 9-inch square pan. Bake at 350°F 30 minutes or until edges just begin to pull away from sides of pan. Cool in pan on a rack. Brush top with a little liqueur if desired. Cool completely before cutting. Cut, with sharp knife, into 1- x 2-inch bars. Makes 2 dozen brownies.

oatmeal chocolate chips *(illustrated opposite)*

Keep the cookie jar filled with these

	1 egg
180 ml	¾ cup brown sugar, packed
5 ml	1 teasp. vanilla
125 ml	½ cup Sunlite Oil
250 ml	1 cup sifted all-purpose flour
3 ml	½ teasp. baking soda
3 ml	½ teasp. salt
250 ml	1 cup quick-cooking oats
250 ml	1 cup semisweet chocolate bits
125 ml	½ cup chopped nuts

In a bowl, beat egg, sugar and vanilla until frothy. Gradually add Sunlite Oil, continuing to beat until well blended. Sift together flour, baking soda and salt; stir into first mixture. Add oats, chocolate bits and nuts; mix well. Drop by rounded teaspoonfuls on ungreased cookie sheet. Bake at 375°F 12 to 15 minutes. Remove and cool on a rack. Makes about 3½ dozen cookies.

doughnuts *(illustrated opposite)*

Soft dough makes for tender results

835 ml	3⅓ cups sifted all-purpose flour
250 ml	1 cup sugar
180 ml	¾ cup milk
30 ml	2 Tablesp. Sunlite Oil
15 ml	1 Tablesp. baking powder
3 ml	½ teasp. salt
	2 eggs

Sift *1½ cups* flour into a large bowl; add *remaining* ingredients and blend on low speed about 30 seconds. Scrape sides of bowl constantly with rubber spatula. Beat on medium speed 2 minutes, scraping bowl occasionally. Stir in *remaining* flour. Turn out on well-floured board; roll to lightly coat; roll out to ⅜-inch thickness. Cut with floured doughnut cutter. Fill a large heavy kettle or Dutch oven ⅓ full with Sunlite Oil. Heat to 375°F and maintain temperature with deep-fry thermometer. Slide doughnuts into hot oil with wide spatula. Turn doughnuts as they rise to surface; turn often until golden brown. Remove from oil; drain on paper towels. Serve plain, cinnamon-sugared or glazed with powdered sugar and dipped in nuts, coconut or cake decorating sprinkles. Makes 2 dozen.

sunlite stir'n'roll pastry

So quick and easy, tender and flaky

For single crust:

335 ml	1⅓ cups sifted all-purpose flour
5 ml	1 teasp. salt
85 ml	⅓ cup Sunlite Oil
45 ml	3 Tablesp. cold milk

For double crust:

500 ml	2 cups sifted all-purpose flour
8 ml	1½ teasp. salt
125 ml	½ cup Sunlite Oil
60 ml	¼ cup cold milk

Mix flour and salt in a medium bowl. Pour Sunlite Oil and milk into one measuring cup (but don't stir). Add all at once to flour; stir until mixed. Press into smooth ball; flatten slightly. (For double crust form into 2 balls.) Place between 2 sheets of wax paper 12 inches square. (Dampen table top to prevent slipping). Roll out gently to edges of paper. Peel off top paper. If dough tears, mend without moistening. Place paper-side up in 8- or 9-inch pie pan. Peel off paper. Ease and fit pastry into pan; trim and flute edge. Prick with fork. Bake at 450°F 10 to 12 minutes until golden brown. (Do not prick if filled before baking).

Note: Follow recipe directions for filling and baking double-crust pies.

berry pie

Boysenberry, blackberry or raspberry

	1 recipe Sunlite double-crust Pastry (above)
450 g	1 (16-oz.) bag frozen, unsweetened berries
170 ml	⅔ cup sugar
85 ml	⅓ cup flour

Prepare dough; divide into 2 balls. Roll out between wax paper; fit one into 8-inch pie pan as recipe directs, allowing 1-inch overhang; cut the other into ½-inch-wide strips. In a bowl, combine berries, sugar and flour; pour into pastry lined pie pan. Arrange pastry strips lattice-fashion over top; trim ends. Fold lower crust over ends of strips; flute. Bake at 425°F 40 to 50 minutes. Makes 6 servings.

68

banana nut bread

Stays marvelously moist for days

430 ml	1¾ cups sifted all-purpose flour
10 ml	2 teasp. baking powder
3 ml	½ teasp. salt
1 ml	¼ teasp. baking soda
170 ml	⅔ cup sugar
	2 eggs, well beaten
85 ml	⅓ cup Sunlite Oil
	2 to 3 very ripe bananas, mashed smooth
250 ml	1 cup finely chopped walnuts

Combine *dry* ingredients in a bowl; add eggs, Sunlite Oil and bananas; beat until smooth. Stir in walnuts. Pour into a greased and floured 9 × 5 × 3-inch loaf pan. Bake at 350°F 60 to 65 minutes until inserted toothpick comes out clean. Makes 1 loaf.

pecan tarts

A Southern classic

	1 recipe Sunlite double-crust Pastry (p. 68)
	3 eggs
180 ml	¾ cup sugar
180 ml	¾ cup dark corn syrup
30 ml	2 Tablesp. Sunlite Oil
5 ml	1 teasp. vanilla
375 ml	1½ cups pecan halves or broken pieces

Prepare dough; divide into 8 balls. Roll out each between wax paper to 5 inches in diameter. Ease and fit into 4-inch tart tins; trim even with top. In a large bowl, beat eggs with wire whip; add *remaining* ingredients *except* pecans; beat until well mixed. Stir in pecans; pour into shells. Bake on cookie sheet at 375°F 25 to 30 minutes. Makes 8 tarts.

french custard pie *(illustrated opposite)*

Impressive for company

125 ml	½ cup sugar
45 ml	3 Tablesp. cornstarch
	Dash salt
500 ml	2 cups milk
	2 eggs, slightly beaten
8 ml	1½ teasp. vanilla
	1 (9-inch) baked Sunlite single crust (p. 68)
750 ml	2 to 3 cups fresh fruit slices or sections (kiwi slices, strawberry slices, pineapple chunks, orange sections, seedless grapes, etc.)

Combine sugar, cornstarch and salt in a saucepan. Add milk, gradually, stirring until mixture is smooth. Bring to boil, stirring constantly; cook about 5 minutes until thick and smooth; stir frequently. Add small amount to eggs in a small bowl; mix well; pour back into saucepan, stirring to blend smoothly. Cook 1 to 2 minutes longer until thick and smooth. Stir in vanilla. Cover surface with wax paper; cool completely. Pour into pie shell; chill. Just before serving, decorate top of pie with fresh fruit. Makes 8 servings.

sunlite carrot cake *(illustrated opposite)*

Old-fashion baked-in flavor

375 ml	1½ cups sugar
375 ml	1½ cups Sunlite Oil
	3 eggs
10 ml	2 teasp. vanilla
500 ml	2 cups sifted all-purpose flour
10 ml	2 teasp. cinnamon
10 ml	2 teasp. baking soda
5 ml	1 teasp. salt
500 ml	2 cups shredded carrots
200 g	1 (7-oz.) pkg. flake coconut
250 ml	1 cup crushed canned pineapple
250 ml	1 cup chopped nuts

In a large bowl, combine sugar, Sunlite Oil, eggs and vanilla; mix thoroughly. Sift together flour, cinnamon, baking soda and salt. Add to first mixture; blend thoroughly. Stir in *remaining* ingredients until well mixed. Pour into greased and floured 13 × 9 × 2-inch pan. Bake at 350°F 50 to 60 minutes until center of cake is firm to the touch. Cool in pan on a rack. Serve plain or frost as desired. Makes 15 servings.

two egg chiffon cake

Moist, delicate layers

	2 eggs, separated
375 ml	1½ cups sugar
560 ml	2¼ cups sifted cake flour
15 ml	3 teasp. baking powder
5 ml	1 teasp. salt
85 ml	⅓ cup Sunlite Oil
250 ml	1 cup milk
8 ml	1½ teasp. vanilla

Beat egg whites until frothy. Gradually add ½ *cup* sugar. Continue beating until mixture is a very stiff and glossy meringue; set aside. Sift *remaining* sugar, flour, baking powder and salt into another bowl. Add Sunlite Oil, *half* the milk and vanilla. Beat 1 minute, medium speed on mixer or 150 vigorous strokes by hand. Scrape sides and bottom of bowl constantly. Add *remaining* milk and egg *yolks*. Beat 1 minute longer, scraping bowl constantly. Fold in meringue. Pour into 2 (8-inch) greased and lightly floured layer-cake pans. Bake at 350°F 30 to 35 minutes; cool slightly; turn out on a rack to cool completely. Frost as desired. Makes 1 (2-layer) cake.

strawberry shortcake

Fresh-baked pastry, stir and bake quick

500 ml	2 cups sifted all-purpose flour
30 ml	2 Tablesp. sugar
15 ml	1 Tablesp. baking powder
5 ml	1 teasp. salt
125 ml	½ cup Sunlite Oil
170 ml	⅔ cup milk
	1 egg yolk, slightly beaten
500 ml	2 cups sour cream
60 ml	¼ cup light brown sugar, packed
1000 ml	4 cups sliced strawberries, sliced peaches or blueberries

Sift dry ingredients together in a large bowl. Pour Sunlite Oil and milk into measuring cup (but don't stir). Then pour all at once into flour; add egg yolk and stir until mixed. Smooth by kneading dough in bowl about 10 times. Drop in 8 equal portions on ungreased cookie sheet. Bake 10 to 12 minutes at 475°F. Meanwhile, place sour cream in small mixing bowl and place in freezer with beaters. (*Don't* leave in freezer *longer than* 20 minutes). Beat sour cream and brown sugar with electric mixer 5 minutes or until double in volume. Split warm shortcakes in half. Fill and top with fruit and sweetened sour cream. Makes 8 servings.

sour cream chocolate cake

Grandmother's best chocolate cake

500 ml	2	cups sifted all-purpose flour
500 ml	2	cups sugar
250 ml	1	cup water
180 ml	¾	cup sour cream
125 ml	½	cup Sunlite Oil
10 ml	2	teasp. baking powder
5 ml	1	teasp. salt
	2	eggs
5 ml	1	teasp. vanilla
110 g	4	ozs. unsweetened chocolate, melted and cooled

Combine *all ingredients* in large mixing bowl. Beat on *low* speed 30 seconds, scraping bowl constantly with rubber spatula. Beat on *high* speed 3 minutes, scraping bowl occasionally. Pour into 2 (9-inch) round or 1 (13 × 9 × 2-inch) pan, greased and floured. Bake at 350°F 30 to 35 minutes for layers; 40 to 45 minutes for rectangular cake until top springs back when touched lightly. Cool 10 minutes in pans on a rack. Remove from pans; cool completely on rack. Frost as desired. Makes 2 (9-inch) layers or 1 (13 × 9 × 2-inch) cake.

zucchini bread *(illustrated page 67)*

Pretty enough for party sandwiches

430 ml	1¾	cups sifted all-purpose flour
125 ml	½	cup sugar
5 ml	1	teasp. baking powder
3 ml	½	teasp. salt
1 ml	¼	teasp. baking soda
125 ml	½	cup Sunlite Oil
250 ml	1	cup grated, unpeeled zucchini
	2	eggs, slightly beaten
60 ml	¼	cup milk

Combine *first* 5 ingredients in a large mixing bowl; stir to mix. Add Sunlite Oil, zucchini, eggs and milk; stir until all ingredients are just blended. Spread evenly in greased and floured (8 × 3 × 2-inch) loaf pan. Bake at 350°F 50 to 55 minutes until toothpick inserted in center comes out clean. Cool in pan on rack 10 minutes. Remove from pan; cool completely on a rack. Makes 1 loaf.

fabulous holiday classics

Elegant main dishes and all the trimmings

crown roast with fruit 'n' rice stuffing

(illustrated opposite)

Elegant alternative to ham or turkey

4500 g	1	(about 10-lb.) 12- to 16-rib crown pork roast
		Salt and pepper
		Apple cider
750 ml	3	cups rice
250 ml	1	cup chopped onion
250 ml	1	cup chopped celery
125 ml	½	cup slivered almonds
180 ml	¾	cup Sunlite Oil
225 g	1	(8-oz.) pkg. mixed dried fruits, chopped coarsely
1500 ml	6	cups chicken broth
15 ml	1	Tablesp. salt
8 ml	1½	teasp. marjoram

Remove all fat from inside of roast. Place, bones up, in a shallow roasting pan. Season with salt and pepper. Insert meat thermometer into meatiest section. Cover exposed bones with foil; crumple additional foil into center to retain shape. Roast at 325°F 3 to 3½ hours or until thermometer reaches 170°F; baste every 45 minutes using ¾ *cup* apple cider and pan juices. Meanwhile, sauté rice, onion, celery and almonds in Sunlite Oil in a Dutch oven until rice is lightly browned. Stir in fruit, broth, *2 cups* apple cider and seasonings. Bring to a boil. Bake, covered, in oven last 45 minutes. To serve, spoon part of rice into center of roast. Makes 12 to 16 servings.

heirloom apple bread

Great for gift giving

625 ml	2½	cups sifted all-purpose flour
10 ml	2	teasp. each: baking powder and baking soda
5 ml	1	teasp. pumpkin pie spice
170 ml	⅔	cup sugar
250 ml	1	cup each: chopped pecans and currants
125 ml	½	cup Sunlite Oil
	2	eggs, slightly beaten
22 ml	1½	Tablesp. vanilla
10 ml	2	teasp. rum extract
	2	medium apples, grated
15 ml	1	Tablesp. grated orange peel
		Pecan halves and strips of orange peel

In a bowl, combine dry ingredients, pecans and currants. Add Sunlite Oil, eggs, vanilla and rum extract; stir just until blended. Fold in apple and orange peel. Spoon into greased and floured 9 × 5 × 3-inch loaf pan; decorate top with pecans and orange peel. Bake at 350°F 55 to 65 minutes until toothpick comes out clean. Cool; refrigerate. Makes 1 loaf.

buffet star ham

Use up those extra Easter eggs

4500 g	1	(10-lb.) fully cooked, boneless ham
	1	egg at room temperature
1 ml	¼	teasp. seasoned salt
15 ml	1	Tablesp. lemon juice
125 ml	½	cup Sunlite Oil at room temperature
250 ml	1	cup creamed cottage cheese
450 g	2	(8-oz.) pkgs. cream cheese, softened
45 ml	3	Tablesp. prepared mustard
	6	hard cooked egg *whites,* shredded
		Green pepper strips, cut 1/16-inch wide
		Pitted ripe olives, sliced into thin wedges
		Watercress

If ham has casing, blanch in boiling water and pull off. Remove as much surface fat as possible; dry ham with paper towel. Chill thoroughly. In a blender jar, blend egg, seasoned salt, lemon juice and *2 tablespoons* Sunlite Oil until mixture begins to thicken. Slowly pour in *remaining* Sunlite Oil while blending until thick and smooth. Blend in cottage cheese until smooth. Combine in a bowl with cream cheese and mustard; mix well. Place ham on serving platter. Spread cheese mixture on top and sides. Sprinkle egg whites evenly over cheese mixture; press in lightly. Decorate ham with "flowers" using green pepper and olives. Refrigerate at least 1½ hours. Surround ham with watercress just before serving. Makes 25 to 30 servings.

waldorf in pineapple boats

Holidays deserve something extra . . .

	1	medium, fresh pineapple
500 ml	2	cups diced red-skinned apples
125 ml	½	cup coarsely chopped celery
125 ml	½	cup golden raisins
60 ml	¼	cup coarsely chopped walnuts
15 ml	1	Tablesp. lemon juice
250 ml	1	cup non-dairy whipped topping
125 ml	½	cup Sunlite Mayonnaise (p. 15)
1 ml	¼	teasp. dried, ground orange peel

Cut pineapple lengthwise into six wedges. Remove meat, leaving ½-inch-thick shells; dice *2 cups* into large bowl. Add apples, celery, raisins, walnuts and lemon juice; toss to mix well. Blend whipped topping, Sunlite Mayonnaise and orange peel in a small bowl; stir into fruit and nut mixture. Chill. Arrange pineapple "boats" on lettuce leaves; fill with salad. Garnish with any remaining fresh pineapple and mint leaves, if desired. Makes 6 generous servings.

chocolate mousse roll

Absolutely smashing!

	6	eggs
250 ml	1	cup sugar
250 ml	1	cup sifted all-purpose flour
85 ml	⅓	cup Sunlite Oil
15 ml	1	Tablesp. water
5 ml	1	teasp. vanilla
		Powdered sugar
250 ml	1	cup whipping cream
85 ml	⅓	cup chocolate-flavored drink mix
		Orange cognac brandy
60 ml	¼	cup sliced toasted almonds

In a large mixing bowl, combine eggs and sugar, stirring until just blended. Set bowl over a large saucepan of hot (not boiling) water. (Be sure water does not touch the bottom of bowl.) Cook over low heat about 10 minutes until egg mixture is lukewarm, stirring occasionally. Remove from heat; beat at high speed 15 minutes, until mixture is tripled in bulk and looks like whipped cream. Slowly sift flour, ¼ *cup at a time,* over the whipped mixture and fold in gently. Carefully drizzle Sunlite Oil, water and vanilla over whipped mixture; fold in gently. Pour into greased and floured 11 × 16-inch jelly roll pan. Bake at 350°F 25 to 30 minutes, until cake pulls away from sides of pan and top springs back when lightly touched. Immediately invert onto a clean towel that has been dusted with powdered sugar; roll up, starting with narrow end; set aside. In a small mixing bowl, blend whipping cream, chocolate drink mix and *2 teaspoons* orange brandy; beat on high speed until soft peaks form. Unroll cooled cake carefully and sprinkle surface with *1 to 2 tablespoons* orange brandy. Spread *half* of whipped cream mixture evenly over cake; reroll. Frost outside with *remaining* whipped mixture. Garnish with almonds; refrigerate. Makes 12 servings.

For an easy, delicious variation, fill the cake with *1 cup* of your favorite jelly or preserves. Reroll the cake; sprinkle with powdered sugar.

roast turkey and corn bread stuffing

Garnish platter with cranberry relish in orange cups

6300 g	12	to 14-lb. turkey
		Sunlite Oil
		Salt and pepper
340 g	1	(12-oz.) pkg. seasoned corn bread stuffing
375 ml	1½	cups chopped celery
250 ml	1	cup minced onion
30 ml	2	Tablesp. minced parsley
250 ml	1	cup broth (from cooking giblets) or water

Rinse turkey and wipe dry; rub with Sunlite Oil, then with salt and pepper. In a large bowl, combine stuffing mix with ½ cup Sunlite Oil and vegetables; stir in broth; mix lightly. Stuff loosely into neck and body cavities. Skewer neck skin to back; tuck legs under skin band; twist wings under turkey. Place turkey, breast-side up, on a rack in a shallow roasting pan. Place a "tent" of foil loosely over turkey. Roast at 325°F 3½ to 4 hours (180° to 185°F on meat thermometer). Remove foil last half hour of roasting. Bake any extra stuffing in a greased, covered casserole dish last 45 minutes of roasting time. Makes 12 to 15 servings of stuffing and turkey.

---

sinfully delicious sweet potato pie

Better than pumpkin pie, some say

	2	medium sweet potatoes, cooked or 1 (29-oz.) can sweet potatoes, drained
180 ml	¾	cup brown sugar, packed
	2	eggs
30 ml	2	Tablesp. Sunlite Oil
250 ml	1	cup evaporated milk
60 ml	¼	cup golden rum (optional)
5 ml	1	teasp. flour
5 ml	1	teasp. cinnamon
3 ml	½	teasp. salt
1 ml	¼	teasp. nutmeg
.5 ml	⅛	teasp. allspice
23 cm	1	(9-inch) unbaked Sunlite single crust (p. 68)

In a bowl, beat sweet potatoes with electric mixer until smooth; remove strings. Measure out *2 cups;* combine with sugar, eggs and Sunlite Oil; mix well. Stir in milk, rum, flour and seasonings; blend thoroughly. Pour into pie shell. Bake at 450°F 15 minutes. *Reduce heat* to 350°F; bake 45 minutes longer. Cool at least 10 minutes before cutting. Makes 1 (9-inch) pie.

family favorite fruitcake (Illustrated page 74)

Sure to become a treasured recipe

250 ml	1	cup Sunlite Oil
375 ml	1½	cups brown sugar, packed
	4	eggs
750 ml	3	cups sifted all-purpose flour
10 ml	2	teasp. salt
5 ml	1	teasp. baking powder
10 ml	2	teasp. each: cinnamon and allspice
5 ml	1	teasp. ground cloves
250 ml	1	cup pineapple, apple or orange juice
250 ml	1	cup thinly sliced citron
250 ml	1	cup chopped candied pineapple
375 ml	1½	cups whole candied cherries
250 ml	1	cup raisins
250 ml	1	cup chopped figs
750 ml	3	cups coarsely chopped nuts

In a large bowl, combine Sunlite Oil, sugar and eggs; beat vigorously with spoon or electric mixer for 2 minutes. Sift *2 cups* of flour with salt, baking powder and spices. Stir into oil mixture alternately with fruit juice. Mix *remaining* cup of flour with fruits and nuts in a large bowl; pour batter over; mix thoroughly. Turn into 2 (9 x 5 x 3-inch) loaf pans greased and lined with brown paper *or* well-greased and floured 12-cup Bundt or tube pan. Place a pan of water on lower oven rack. Bake on rack above pan of water at 275°F about 2½ hours until a toothpick inserted in center comes out clean. After baking, let cakes stand 15 minutes before removing from pans. Cool thoroughly on racks without removing paper. When cool, remove paper; wrap in aluminum foil; store to ripen. If desired, cakes can be wrapped in cloth dampened with brandy or wine. When ready to serve, glaze or garnish as desired. To aid in slicing, chill cake in the refrigerator an hour or two. Makes about 6 lbs. of fruitcake (2 loaves or 1 round).

creative cookery for two

A potpourri of scrumptious dishes scaled for mini-families

stuffed lamb breast *(illustrated opposite)*

Elegant and inexpensive

60 ml	¼ cup <u>each:</u> chopped celery and onion
	Sunlite Oil
375 ml	1 to 1½ cups seasoned stuffing mix
60 ml	¼ cup water
1 ml	¼ teasp. pepper
	1 clove garlic, crushed
1 ml	¼ teasp. oregano
1 ml	¼ teasp. seasoned salt
450 g	1 lb. lamb breast with pocket

In medium skillet, sauté celery and onions in *2 tablespoons* Sunlite Oil until tender. Blend in stuffing mix, water and pepper; set aside. In a small bowl, blend *1 tablespoon* Sunlite Oil with garlic, oregano and seasoned salt. Rub lamb breast inside and out with seasoned mixture; fill pocket with stuffing; secure with toothpicks. Place in shallow baking dish; bake at 450°F 15 minutes, *reduce heat* to 350°F; bake *30 minutes longer.* Makes 2 servings.

ham rolls au gratin

Impress your guest

	6 medium mushrooms, chopped
60 ml	¼ cup chopped onion
	Sunlite Oil
284 g	1 (10-oz.) pkg. frozen asparagus spears
	4 thin slices ham
30 ml	2 Tablesp. flour
3 ml	½ teasp. seasoned salt
.5 ml	⅛ teasp. pepper
310 ml	1¼ cups milk
60 ml	¼ cup grated Swiss or Gruyère cheese

In a medium skillet, sauté mushrooms and onions in *2 tablespoons* Sunlite Oil until tender. Place equal portions of mushroom mixture and asparagus spears down center of each ham slice; roll ham to wrap stuffing; place seam-side down in center of baking dish. Bake, covered, at 325°F 20 to 25 minutes. Meanwhile, in a saucepan, cook flour in *2 tablespoons* Sunlite Oil until golden; add spices; blend in milk slowly. Cook over medium heat, stirring, until smooth and slightly thickened. Add cheese; stir until melted. To serve, top ham rolls with cheese sauce. Makes 2 servings.

three tempting chicken dinners

Start with a 3-lb. whole or cut-up frying chicken.
If whole-body, cut into pieces as shown below.

Pound for pound, a whole chicken is less expensive than buying by the piece. Cut the chicken into pieces shown in the diagram. Wrap and freeze portions for three different meals.

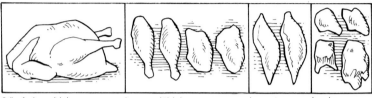

3-lb. frying chicken   legs and thighs   breast halves   backs, wings and neck

Use legs and thighs for one dinner: fry, barbecue or in recipe below.

Use breast halves for second dinner: sauté, chicken kiev or in stir-fry (opposite page).

For third dinner, cook or steam backs, neck and wings in small amount of salted water 20 to 25 minutes until tender. Remove meat, discard skin and bones, dice meat and use in recipes like the one opposite calling for cooked chicken.

dinner in a skillet

One-dish dinner, stove-top quick

	2	each: chicken thighs and legs
		Salt and pepper
45 ml	3	Tablesp. Sunlite Oil
125 ml	½	cup chopped onion
85 ml	⅓	cup rice
	4	mushrooms, sliced
	2	ribs celery, sliced
298 g	1	(10½-oz.) can cream of mushroom soup
125 ml	½	cup water
125 ml	½	cup frozen peas
30 ml	2	Tablesp. chopped pimiento

Season chicken with salt and pepper. Brown 5 minutes on each side in a skillet in Sunlite Oil; remove from skillet. Add onion, rice, mushrooms and celery to skillet; sauté until onion is transparent. Stir in soup and water; arrange browned chicken over top. Cook, covered, over *low* heat 30 to 35 minutes; add peas and pimiento last 10 minutes of cooking. Makes 2 servings.

summer stir-fry

	2 chicken breast halves, boned and skinned
	Sunlite Oil
60 ml	¼ cup each: cut asparagus spears, sliced celery, carrots, onions, zucchini and summer squash
250 ml	1 cup chicken broth
15 ml	1 Tablesp. each: cornstarch and soy sauce mixed with ¼ cup cold water
1 ml	¼ teasp. each: ginger and garlic powder
	Chow mein noodles

Cut chicken in 2-inch strips. Stir and fry in a wok or 12-inch skillet, in *1 tablespoon* Sunlite Oil until golden. Remove from pan. Heat *1 more tablespoon* Sunlite Oil, add vegetables; stir and fry until just crisp-tender. Push vegetables up on sides of wok, add broth, cornstarch mixture, seasonings and chicken. Cook and stir until glossy. Serve over noodles. Makes 2 servings.

chicken en casserole

125 ml	½ cup each: diced onion and green pepper
30 ml	2 Tablesp. Sunlite Oil
298 g	1 (10½-oz.) can cream of celery soup
250 ml	1 cup diced cooked chicken
250 ml	1 cup cooked noodles
30 ml	2 Tablesp. each: dry sherry and diced pimiento
3 ml	½ teasp. garlic salt
1 ml	¼ teasp. pepper
250 ml	1 cup shredded Cheddar cheese
	Fine, dry bread crumbs

In a skillet, sauté onions and green pepper in Sunlite Oil until tender. Add remaining ingredients *except* bread crumbs; mix thoroughly. Bring to boil. Spoon into two individual casserole dishes; top with bread crumbs. Broil, 4 inches from source of heat, until golden brown. Makes 2 servings.

pork tetrazzini

Richly sauced in the Continental manner

	4 large mushrooms, sliced
60 ml	¼ cup diced onion
60 ml	¼ cup Sunlite Oil
45 ml	3 Tablesp. flour
375 ml	1½ cups milk
250 ml	1 cup cubed cooked pork or other meat
3 ml	½ teasp. seasoned salt
.5 ml	⅛ teasp. each: garlic salt, pepper and nutmeg
60 ml	¼ cup dry white wine
110 g	½ (8-oz.) pkg. noodles, cooked and drained
30 ml	2 Tablesp. grated Parmesan cheese
	Minced parsley (optional)

In a medium skillet, sauté mushrooms and onions in Sunlite Oil until tender; stir in flour until smooth; cook 2 to 3 minutes. Add milk gradually, stirring constantly; stir in pork and seasonings; cook 5 minutes longer, stirring, until slightly thickened. In a small bowl, add a little warm sauce to wine, stirring constantly. Return to rest of sauce; heat until "bubbly." Arrange *equal* portions of hot, cooked noodles in 2 individual casseroles; spoon over equal portions of meat and sauce; sprinkle with Parmesan cheese and parsley. Makes 2 servings.

tacos

Macho meal pleaser

225 g	½ lb. ground beef
60 ml	¼ cup chopped onion
60 ml	¼ cup water
5 ml	1 teasp. chili powder
3 ml	½ teasp. salt
.5 ml	⅛ teasp. each: pepper and cumin
	Dash Tabasco
	4 corn tortillas
	Sunlite Oil
250 ml	1 cup shredded lettuce
125 ml	½ cup chopped tomato
125 ml	½ cup shredded Cheddar cheese

In a medium skillet, sauté ground beef and onion until beef loses redness; drain excess fat. Add water and seasonings; simmer over medium heat 3 to 5 minutes; stir occasionally. Meanwhile, heat ¼ inch Sunlite Oil in a heavy skillet. Fry tortillas quickly on both sides. Fold in half; remove from skillet. Drain on paper towels. Fill each taco with equal amounts of ground beef mixture; top with lettuce, tomato and cheese. Makes 4 tacos.

elegant beef wellington duo

The perfect dinner for two

225 g	½	lb. extra lean ground beef
125 ml	½	cup fine, dry bread crumbs
	1	egg, separated
15 ml	1	Tablesp. prepared horseradish
3 ml	½	teasp. salt
225 g	1	(8-oz.) can tomato sauce
	1	recipe Sunlite single-crust Pastry (p.68)
		Wine Sauce (recipe follows)

Combine in a medium bowl, ground beef, bread crumbs, egg *yolk,* horseradish, salt and ¼ *cup* tomato sauce. Shape mixture into 2 rectangular loaves. Bake on a rack in a shallow baking pan at 400°F 15 minutes. Cool on rack 5 to 10 minutes. Meanwhile, prepare dough. Roll into 2 rectangles, between wax paper large enough to wrap around loaves; peel off top paper; place loaves in center of each pastry. Wrap pastry around, overlapping edges on bottom. Trim off excess pastry at ends. Moisten edges and pinch together to seal. Make decorative cutouts from excess pastry and arrange on top of each loaf. Place on ungreased baking pan. Brush entire surface with egg *white* mixed with a little water. Bake at 400°F 20 minutes longer. Serve with Wine Sauce. Makes 2 servings.

Wine Sauce: Combine *remaining* tomato sauce, ¼ cup wine and 2 tablespoons <u>each</u>: brown sugar, lemon juice and Worcestershire and ⅛ teaspoon crushed tarragon. Simmer over low heat about 10 minutes.

tuna melt

Dill weed makes the difference

98 g	1	(3½-oz.) can water packed tuna, drained
60 ml	¼	cup Sunlite Mayonnaise (p.15)
15 ml	1	Tablesp. diced green onion
8 ml	1½	teasp. dill weed
8 ml	1½	teasp. sweet pickle relish
1 ml	¼	teasp. seasoned salt
	4	slices sourdough bread
	4	slices Cheddar cheese
	4	slices tomato
		Margarine

In a medium bowl, combine tuna with Sunlite Mayonnaise, onion, dill weed, pickle relish and salt; mix well. Layer *2 slices* bread with equal portions tuna mixture, cheese and tomato slices; top each with *remaining* bread slices. Spread *both* sides of sandwiches lightly with margarine. In a large skillet, grill sandwiches over medium heat. Cover to heat filling and melt cheese. Makes 2 sandwiches.

four hearty beef dinners

One economical roast is the secret

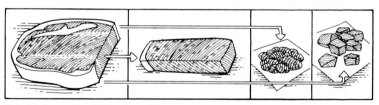

(3-lb.) 7-Bone Chuck Roast   Roast   Chopped for   Cubed for
                                          chili meat   stew meat

Start with a (3-lb.) 7-bone chuck beef roast.

Cut across the roast *beneath* the 7-bone. Remove the bone and cut the meat into cubes for stew or strips for stroganoff.

Cut across the roast at the natural separation *below* the center larger portion of the roast. Use this for a pot roast.

Remove the bone from the *remaining* portion of the roast. Chop the meat coarsely for making chili or soup.

beef bourguignonne

Serve with hot noodles tossed with poppy seeds

		Roast (as shown in diagram above)*
		Salt, pepper and paprika
22 ml	1½	Tablesp. Sunlite Oil
125 ml	½	cup water
85 ml	⅓	cup burgundy wine
	2	carrots, cut in 1-inch pieces
	5	boiling onions

Rub roast generously with salt, pepper and paprika. Brown on both sides in an oven-proof skillet in Sunlite Oil. Add water and wine; roast, covered, at 350°F 45 minutes. Add carrots and onions; roast, covered, 45 minutes longer. Makes 2 servings.

*Add bones (cut from roast) to skillet for added flavor. Discard when roast is cooked.

texas chili

	Chopped meat (as shown in diagram p. 86)
125 ml	½ cup chopped onion
30 ml	2 Tablesp. Sunlite Oil
22 ml	1½ Tablesp. chili powder
5 ml	1 teasp. each: cumin and paprika
5 ml	1 teasp. garlic salt
3 ml	½ teasp. ground oregano
214 g	1 (7½-oz.) can whole tomatoes
125 ml	½ cup water
	1 beef bouillon cube

In a large skillet, brown meat and onion in Sunlite Oil. Add *remaining* ingredients; stir until well mixed. Simmer, covered, 1 hour; stir occasionally Makes 2 servings.

country-style beef stew

	Stew meat (as shown in diagram p. 86)
30 ml	2 Tablesp. flour
	1 small onion, quartered
	1 clove garlic, minced
30 ml	2 Tablesp. Sunlite Oil
225 g	1 (8-oz.) can tomato sauce
250 ml	1 cup water
	1 bay leaf
3 ml	½ teasp. seasoned salt
.5 ml	⅛ teasp. pepper
	2 large carrots, quartered
	1 large potato, peeled and cut into eighths

Dredge meat in flour. In a heavy skillet, brown meat, onions and garlic in Sunlite Oil. Add remaining ingredients, *except:* carrots and potatoes. Simmer, covered, 1½ hours; stir occasionally. Remove bay leaf; add vegetables and simmer, covered, 40 minutes longer. Makes 2 servings.

hearty beef hash

375 ml	1½ cups frozen hash brown potatoes
125 ml	½ cup diced cooked beef (left over from roast)
60 ml	¼ cup chopped onion
30 ml	2 Tablesp. Sunlite Oil
3 ml	½ teasp. salt
1 ml	¼ teasp. pepper

In a medium skillet, fry hashbrowns, beef and onions in Sunlite Oil 6 to 8 minutes; sprinkle with salt and pepper. Makes 2 servings.

onion soup au gratin

Serve with crusty French bread and spinach salad

	1	large sweet Bermuda onion, thinly sliced and separated into rings
30 ml	2	Tablesp. Sunlite Oil
284 g	1	(10 oz.) can each: beef broth and water
	2	slices sourdough bread, toasted
30 ml	2	Tablesp. grated Parmesan cheese
250 ml	1	cup shredded mozzarella cheese

In a saucepan, sauté onions in Sunlite Oil until transparent and golden in color. Add broth and water; simmer, covered, 15 minutes. Place toast in bottom of 2 individual, 1½-cup oven-proof soup crocks or casseroles. Top with equal portions Parmesan. Add onions and broth; layer mozzarella over top of each. Place under broiler, 4 inches from source of heat, until top bubbles and crust forms. Makes 2 servings.

biscuits for two

Stir-'n'-roll quick, fresh-baked good

250 ml	1	cup sifted flour
8 ml	1½	teasp. baking powder
3 ml	½	teasp. salt
85 ml	⅓	cup milk
45 ml	3	Tablesp. Sunlite Oil

In a medium bowl, sift dry ingredients. Pour milk and Sunlite Oil into one measuring cup; *do not mix.* Pour all at once into flour mixture. Stir with fork until mixture forms ball. Roll out ½-inch thick between sheets of wax paper. (Dampen tabletop to prevent slipping.) Cut with 2-inch biscuit cutter. Bake on an ungreased baking sheet at 475°F 10 to 15 minutes. Makes 6 biscuits.

old-fashioned berry shortcake

	1	recipe Sunlite Biscuits for Two (recipe above)
		Sugar
500 ml	2	cups berries in season
		Whipped or light cream

Prepare biscuits according to directions, *adding 1 tablespoon* sugar. Cut into 2 large biscuits; bake at 475°F 15 minutes. Meanwhile, in a small bowl, combine berries with *1 tablespoon* sugar; mash slightly; chill. To serve, split warm biscuits; place on individual serving plates. Spoon berries between and over top of each. Serve with whipped or light cream, as desired. Makes 2 servings.

daily guide to eating ``lite´´

A sense of well-being includes looking great and feeling good. Watching your daily food intake and exercising on a regular basis are important to feeling right.

Eating wisely can be learned. Be more selective when you're planning meals, shopping and cooking. A real satisfaction comes when you experience the joy of knowing that you are eating wisely.

First, use the Basic Four Food Groups as a guide to planning your meals. For a balanced meal every day choose from meats, fish and poultry; fruits and vegetables; milk and dairy products; and grain foods.

Discover new ways to include these foods to best suit your family's nutritional needs. And try new methods of preparing them. For instance, steaming or sautéing vegetables seals in their vitamins and minerals.

Try to include more fish and poultry in your meals. They're lower in fat content and, without the skin, they have less saturated fats. Be sure to trim visible fat from red meats and select lean cuts more often.

Select fat-free or low-fat dairy products. These are lower in saturated fats, cholesterol and calories.

Keep fruits, nuts and raw vegetables on hand as refreshing snacks to discourage nibbling on sweets or foods loaded with heavy starches.

Include more grains and pasta. These help stretch your meal budget, they can be used in all sorts of wonderful dishes, and they provide important complex carbohydrates, vitamins and minerals.

When frying and sautéing use Sunlite Oil, a vegetable oil that is high in polyunsaturates rather than butter or solid fats.

So, eat "lite" . . . feel right . . . and enjoy delicious foods prepared with Sunlite, the 100% sunflower oil.

"Enjoy"—Hunt-Wesson Kitchens' Staff
Carolyn Avelino
Delois Brown
Kathleen Dixon
Nancy Freeberg
Kitty O'Connell

the pure joy of sunlite oil

Welcome to the wonderful world of cooking with Sunlite Oil. 100% pure sunflower oil, Sunlite is higher in polyunsaturates than the three leading brands, including corn oil. Cholesterol-free and with no preservatives, its delicate flavor comes shining through in light-tasting, perfectly-dressed salads; crisp, fried chicken and seafood; tender flaky pastry; moist delicate cakes . . . and much more. You cook in a whole new "lite" with Sunlite!

To assure the very best success every time . . .

Sunlite Oil Is Bottled in Convenient Sizes.
Select the size best-suited to your cooking needs. The larger sizes are usually economical if you do a lot of baking and frying, or if you have a large family.

Sunlite Oil Retains Freshness and Flavor.
Just recap tightly after each use and store in a cool, dark cupboard. Refrigeration is not recommended.

Sunlite Oil Will Substitute for Solid Shortening in Most Recipes.
Use measure for measure for melted shortening or fat in batter recipes, sauce rouxs, sautéing or pan-frying.
Use a little less than solid shortening measure in recipes.
As a rule of thumb, use 7 tablespoons of Sunlite Oil for ½ cup solid shortening.

Sunlite Oil Deep-Fries Foods Crispy-Light and Grease-Free.
Fill frying utensil no more than ⅓ full with Sunlite Oil.
Never cover pan when heating oil; never leave unattended.
Use a deep-fry thermometer to check temperature to ensure crisp, perfectly cooked, grease-free results.
Use a frying basket, slotted spoon or tongs when adding or removing food from hot oil.
Lower food gradually into hot oil to prevent spattering.
Before frying moist foods, dry between paper towels.
Drain on paper towels after frying.

Frying Oil Can Be Reused Several Times with Excellent Results.
After each frying, fry a few slices of potato to "sweeten" the oil and remove any off-flavor. Allow oil to cool.
Strain into clean container using a sieve lined with cleaning tissue.
Cover tightly and store in cool, dark place.
Add a little fresh Sunlite Oil each time before frying.

CAUTION
Always follow recommended frying temperature (350° to 375°F).
Overheating any oil or shortening can result in fire. If smoking occurs, turn off heat immediately. In case of fire, smother flames with a lid or other cover. *Never use water or attempt to move utensil.*

sunlite

100% Sunflower Oil

32 FL OZ (1 QT) 946ml

kitchen metrics

With metric packaging a reality, metric recipe and utensil measurements cannot be far behind. We are learning to think of packaged and canned foods we buy as grams of weight as well as ounces and pounds. We buy milk and fruit juices by liters as well as pints, quarts and gallons.

The Sunlite Oil recipes in this book include both the U.S. standard measure or weight and the rounded* metric equivalent for each ingredient. The following basic guide will help you adapt other recipes you use.

When *measuring* ingredients *by volume*

    1 teasp. (teaspoon) = 5 ml (milliliters)
    1 Tablesp. (tablespoon) = 15 ml (milliliters)
    1 cup = 250 ml (milliliters)

When *buying* ingredients *by weight*
    1 oz. (ounce) = 28 g (grams)
    8 ozs. (ounces) = 225 g (grams)
    1 lb. (pound) = 450 g (grams)

Additional measures important to cooking and baking include sizes for saucepans, casseroles and baking pans and many of these now include metric information. For example: *Saucepans and casseroles* usually are measured *by volume content*

    1 qt. (quart) = 1 l (liter)
    1½ qts. (quarts) = 1.5 l (liters)
    ½ gal. (gallon) = 2 l (liters)

Baking pans usually are measured *by diameter or by length, width and depth*
    8-inch pan = 20 cm (centimeters)
    9-inch pan = 23 cm (centimeters)
    10-inch tube pan = 25 cm (centimeters)
    13×9×2-inch pan = 33×23×5 cm (centimeters)
    9×5×3-inch loaf pan = 23×13×8 cm (centimeters)
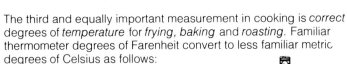

The third and equally important measurement in cooking is *correct* degrees of *temperature* for *frying, baking* and *roasting*. Familiar thermometer degrees of Farenheit convert to less familiar metric degrees of Celsius as follows:

Farenheit degrees		Celsius degrees
250°–275°F	=	120°–135°C
300°–325°F	=	150°–165°C
350°–375°F	=	175°–190°C
400°–425°F	=	205°–220°C
450°–475°F	=	230°–245°C

*Note: Although, for convenience, all metric measures used in recipes in this book have been rounded off, the resulting dish is in no way changed.

index

93

Authors: Hunt-Wesson Home Economists

Carolyn Avelino   Kathleen Dixon   Kitty O'Connell
Delois Brown   Nancy Freeberg

ART DIRECTOR: JANIS GORSVANS
PHOTOGRAPHY: TOM KELLEY
PROJECT COORDINATORS: RICHARD MAGIDSON
CAROLYN AVELINO